SUCCESS WITH
ROSES

SUCCESS WITH
ROSES

Graham Clarke

GUILD OF MASTER CRAFTSMAN
PUBLICATIONS LTD

First published 2007 by
Guild of Master Craftsman Publications Ltd
Castle Place, 166 High Street
Lewes, East Sussex BN7 1XU

ISBN-13: 978-1-86108-464-4
ISBN-10: 1-86108-464-1

Production Manager: Jim Bulley
Managing Editor: Gerrie Purcell
Project Editor: Gill Parris
Managing Art Editor: Gilda Pacitti
Designer: John Hawkins
Illustrator: Penny Brown

Photographic Acknowledgements
All pictures were taken by the author, except for those listed below:
GMC/Eric Sawford: front and back covers, pages 14, 15, 16, 21,
29, 51 (left), 52 (bottom), 58 (right), 62, 92, 102, 105 (bottom), 107
(bottom), 111 (bottom), 112, 113 (top), 115 (bottom), 119 (top right),
120, 121 (top), 124 (top), 126, 127, 132, 133 (top), 135 (top), 138,
139 (top left and top right), 141 (bottom left, top right, bottom right), 142
(all except top right), 143 (second down left, bottom left, top right, bottom
right), 144 (all except bottom right), 145 (all except bottom left), 146
(all except top left and second down right), 147, 149 (left),
150 (both), 151 (both) and 153 (both).
Fryers Roses: 136 (top right).
David Austin Roses: 141 (left centre).

Set in Futura
Colour reproduction by Altaimage
Printed and bound by Sino Publishing in China

Contents

LEFT A rose garden in the Victorian style, comprising neatly planted beds with standards and bush varieties.

ABOVE 'Dortmund' AGM, a low climbing rose with large, single crimson flowers.

Introduction

Even though the rose is generally considered to be the archetypal English flower, it is not exclusive to England. Naturalized (that is, wild) roses are found throughout North America, Asia, North Africa and the whole of Europe – in fact most of the civilized world shares this quintessential and most precious flower.

There are so many different types of rose, that estimates of the number of species and varieties that exist vary. At the last count it was around 150 species, and several thousand varieties worldwide. Garden centres these days stock a good selection, and there are many specialist rose nurseries and suppliers, so that, with careful choosing, you could have colour from roses for nearly nine months of the year if you live in a temperate part of the world.

In the past roses were considered 'high-maintenance' plants. But now there are many varieties that have been bred specifically for resistance against some of the common pests and diseases, and there are even varieties without thorns. There are some excellent fertilizers that are formulated just for roses, and these only need to be applied three or four times a year.

Even pruning bush roses does not need to be as precise now as was once thought. Indeed, trials have shown that, if you go over a rose with a hedge trimmer, you end up with as much flower as if you had spent hours examining a plant and making a slanted, outward-facing pruning cut precisely quarter of an inch (6mm) above a bud, which was the way older gardeners were taught.

So what types are there? In the main they fall into one of these categories: hybrid teas, floribundas, miniature and patio roses, ground-cover roses, climbers and ramblers, and shrub roses. Between them they offer us some of the most eye-catching and glamorous of garden plants at one extreme, and some of the daintiest and most fragile-looking plants at the other.

There are some fabulous images in this book which I hope will encourage you to go out there and buy, but it's essential to choose the right variety for colour, height, scent, soil, or any of the other attributes that you consider important. Follow the advice given in this book to ensure that the roses you choose will be a truly stunning addition to your garden.

AWARD OF GARDEN MERIT

Throughout this book you will see the initials AGM set after certain plants. This denotes that the plant in question has passed certain assessments carried out by experts under the auspices of the Royal Horticultural Society in Great Britain. Only plants with exceptionally good garden qualities can be awarded this special Award of Garden Merit.

LEFT Few gardens today are dedicated
solely to roses; usually they are
components of a mixed garden.

CHAPTER 1

Using roses in the garden

In years gone by, rose enthusiasts tended to create large rose beds or borders where roses were grown to the exclusion of virtually everything else. When the roses were in flower there was a spectacle like no other, but when the roses were not 'in season', the beds appeared at best dull, and at worst – in winter – empty and lifeless. I believe that this, to a large degree, is the reason for the decline in popularity of the rose during the 1990s and early 2000s, when annual sales of roses dropped and many rose nurseries closed.

However, interest in roses is growing again, and this is largely due to the varieties that have been bred for ease of growing. There are now roses for all parts of the garden (shade as well as sun); there are roses without thorns; there are roses that are hardly ever infested with pests or diseases; there are roses that scarcely need pruning; roses for containers, steep banks, inner-city gardens and coastal plots. And then there is the choice of colour, height and intensity of fragrance. Yes, the rose is back!

ABOVE Rose borders, separated by wide grass paths, are a real spectacle – in summer.

MIXED PLANTINGS

Roses are, to all intents and purposes, flowering shrubs. True, they are different in form and habit to the majority of garden shrubs, but you cannot sensibly classify roses as perennial plants (in the style of chrysanthemums or delphiniums), as they are woody, and perennials are not. So, accepting that roses are shrubs, I would like to see more gardeners using them in the same way that they grow other flowering shrubs. That is, to interplant them in decorative borders with herbaceous perennials and mixed with other shrubs – and even with bulbs and annuals, or bedding plants.

I've grown roses mixed with all manner of flowering shrubs, and one of the most alluring combinations, for me at least, was a pink rose 'Queen Elizabeth' poking through a sea of lilac-coloured *Hebe* 'Autumn Glory'. Roses look wonderful when they are planted next to – or between – perennial geraniums (cranesbills). An underplanting of violets, or low-growing annuals such as white alyssum can be breathtakingly different. I've seen tall white lilies appear through a mass of intense red floribunda roses, and the effect was stunning. I've seen standard roses used as 'dot' plants, appearing erect through a mass of bright summer bedding. If you are clever, you could use complementary colours, such as yellow standard roses over blue-flowered ageratum; or pink standards over a mixed carpet of white petunias and silver-leaved *Cineraria maritima*.

ABOVE A flower of rose 'Queen Elizabeth' peeping through a sea of *Hebe* 'Autumn Glory'.

LEFT The pink form of the rose 'Flower Carpet', seen here growing in front of the Houses of Parliament, London, is considered to be one of the best low-maintenance roses of all time.

ABOVE The modern climbing rose 'Meg' is seen at its best when scrambling through large and robust trees, shrubs, or hedges.

The effect of mixed planting can be quite intoxicating, and it is great fun on a winter's evening to plan summer schemes like this.

Roses also mix remarkably well with vegetables, herbs and even fruit, and they are well suited to the potager-style of gardening, where edible plants are grown amongst flowering and decorative plants. A herb garden edged with a low shrub rose can look fantastic, as can a herb garden centrepiece of an obelisk or archway, with climbing roses growing all over it.

Roses are not normally associated with the straight, regimented rows of seedlings in a vegetable garden, but there is no reason on earth why you should not edge or divide the vegetable area with roses.

Of course, the difference between a bed and a border is obvious when you think about it. A bed is effectively an 'island' of plants, usually surrounded by lawn, or paving, or a mixture of grass and hard landscaping. A border, on the other hand, is an area immediately in front of a backdrop, such as a hedge, wall, or boundary fence. Borders are usually long and thin, certainly when compared to a 'bed', but they can also be short and wide. Roses are suitable for both beds and borders: a bed can accommodate a number of roses all at the same height, or you can choose to grow smaller ones at the front, medium-sized ones a little further in, and then the tallest ones in the centre of the bed; but in a border, the tallest varieties should be at the back, or at the very least, set behind shorter plants.

Climbing roses can also be grown with other climbers, but the only one I would recommend combining them with is clematis. Choose clematis in colours to complement those of the rose, and of a form and habit that won't result in the plants strangling each other. Choose those smaller-flowered clematis – such as the many forms of *Clematis viticella* – that flower from mid-summer onwards, and thus require hard pruning. They can then be cut back at the same time as any rose pruning is performed, in early spring.

INDIVIDUAL PLANTINGS

Roses are used far too infrequently as individual specimens. Whilst most of the bush forms, such as hybrid teas and floribundas, may not be the best examples for singling out, many of the larger shrub roses can make superb focal points, centrepieces to larger displays, or as single specimens set in a lawn, for example.

A specimen rose has to be worthy of a place, entirely on its own merits. Let me explain: when roses – or any plants – are grown amongst others, their imperfections are often hidden, or detracted from, by the plants growing next to and around them. For example, the stems of neighbouring plants can obscure unbalanced growth, or lower-growing plants in front can hide bare stems. But a specimen rose has to look good for most of the year, as it is permanently on show. When it's in flower, it should be a thing of unmatched beauty. And when it is out of season, it should still be presentably neat of habit and preferably with secondary interest, such as autumn fruits, known as 'hips', or interesting winter stems, and so on.

This means that you will need to select your specimen rose most carefully, and maintain it rigorously. You should certainly aim to keep it in balance with the area and plants around it. For example, a single bush rose, such as a hybrid tea or floribunda, when planted on its own in the middle of a large lawn, would look incongruous – or just plain silly. Equally, a huge 10ft (3m) high shrub rose in the middle of a tiny courtyard or front garden would be ridiculous.

Standard roses are a favourite choice for specimen planting. A mature, weeping standard rose in full flower, set in a simple, circular bed in

ABOVE The shrub rose 'Nevada', with its lovely cream-white flowers in late spring and early summer, is a good example of a specimen rose.

the middle of a well-kept lawn, is hard to beat. But, as we shall see later in the book, the standard rose need not be weeping – it need not even be a full standard, as half- and miniature standards are also available.

Many shrub roses make excellent individual specimens, where space allows (see pages 138–47). I've seen the wonderful, white, 'Blanc Double de Coubert' set against a dark green conifer hedge. And I've witnessed a specimen of moss rose 'William Lobb' fully flowering its heart out, the purplish-pink double flowers on arched stems reaching almost to the ground. And I've grown the tall, upright 'Frühlingsgold' with golden-yellow petals and slightly deeper yellow stamens; it is a stunner in any garden and in any situation, and it positively demands to be grown on its own.

ABOVE 'Bonica' AGM flowers right through summer and autumn, and is one of the finest and most floriferous of ground-cover roses.

VERTICAL PLANTINGS

Climbing and rambling roses offer a special opportunity for the creative gardener. However, while having climbers festooning your home in traditional cottage-garden style might be appealing, it may not be entirely practicable. Most houses are not cottages, nor do they have a cottage 'style' about them, and so a climbing rose – especially a stiff-stemmed modern variety trained on to a rigid trellis against the wall – can appear incongruous and artificial.

There are more natural ways to display climbing roses: open structures, such as freestanding trellises, are suitable; archways, too, make ideal supports – they can frame a view very effectively, or form the entrance to the garden; pergolas – a series of connected archways through which one walks, or under which one sits – generally have uprights made of stone in large gardens, but in small, modern gardens wooden posts are perfectly adequate (but ensure that the timber has been pressure-treated with non-toxic preservative).

The 'pillar' – simply a post, old tree trunk (preferably not still on its own roots) or similar structure – is one of the most useful yet under-used supports for climbing roses. It should be no taller than 6ft (2m) tall, which makes it perfect for supporting a relatively low-growing climber.

Living trees can also provide excellent supports for climbing roses, especially varieties with softer, more pliable stems: the larger the tree, the more vigorous the rose that may be grown over it. Young trees, and old and frail trees, may be weakened by having to support such additional weight.

It should be noted that climbing roses trained on a wall will always be more prone to mildew. To help prevent this debilitating fungal disease, the trellis or other support should be fixed to battens to lift it from the surface of the wall, to permit as great a circulation of air around the stems and leaves as possible.

ABOVE **'Aloha' AGM is a low-growing modern climber, with rose-pink double blooms, and a strong fragrance.**

ABOVE **'François Juranville' is a tall rambler with bright rose-pink flowers, but only moderate fragrance.**

GROUND-COVER PLANTINGS

Low-growing, spreading roses fall into the 'ground-cover' category. Most form a dense, leafy mat, and the uses to which these prostrate roses can be put in the garden are numerous — for example, hiding unsightly mounds and manhole covers, filling large flat beds, edging rose beds and covering sloping banks.

Growing roses in this way may seem a modern idea, but this is the natural habit of some wild roses, such as *Rosa wichurana*, a natural rose that originated in China, and from which a number of the modern ground-cover roses have been bred.

The best variety of rose for your purposes will depend on the space available: if you have a small patch or narrow strip of ground to cover, use the Japanese rose 'Nozomi' AGM, with its tiny leaves and small, pearly white flowers. Slightly larger and just as suitable is 'Max Graf', which will quickly produce a 5ft (1.5m) mat of green leaves and bright pink flowers.

On the other hand, if there is a large stretch of land to cover, you could consider a rambler rose. The tall-growing older varieties, without

ABOVE Although 'Dortmund' AGM is a modern climber, it can also be used to scramble over banks and unsightly mounds.

their usual supports, can be used in this way. The varieties 'Dorothy Perkins', 'Albéric Barbier' AGM and 'François Juranville' will happily grow along the ground.

A word of warning, however: never regard ground-cover roses as weed eliminators. Planting these roses in soil that is host to couch grass, ground elder or bindweed will leave you with the hopeless task of trying to pull out the weeds from a tangled thorny mass of rose stems. It is important, therefore, that you dig out the roots of perennial weeds before planting ground-cover roses.

ABOVE 'Berkshire' AGM is a ground-cover rose with cherry pink blooms, each with a golden centre.

ROSES IN POTS AND TUBS

Growing roses in containers has become more and more popular, particularly in small patio gardens, courtyards and in front gardens where the amount of available soil to grow roses may be limited. However, it is not every rose that is suitable for growing in a container and, equally, it is not every container that is suitable for housing a rose.

The reason for both of these misgivings boils down to two things: roses develop long roots to reach moisture reserves deep into the ground, and they have a high demand for water. A pot used for growing roses should, therefore, be relatively deep in relation to its width, and the pot should be checked for watering very regularly. See more 'dos and don'ts' overleaf.

ABOVE 'Flower Carpet' – in this instance the pink form – can be trained into a standard, and grown in a container.

ABOVE **A range of pots and tubs is available, but make sure they are deep enough to accommodate the roots of roses.**

ABOVE **Modern containers can be very decorative, but you should choose carefully, as not all styles will be suitable for roses.**

◆ Do not grow any of the larger types of roses in a container; choose miniature or patio roses (see pages 94–101), as the diminutive features of these roses are shown off to best advantage in this way.

◆ Use 8in (20cm) pots – not smaller – made of terracotta, not plastic. Terracotta is a wonderful material: not only does it look better than plastic, particularly as it ages, but it also seems to provide the correct balance of aeration and moisture-retention that rose roots need.

◆ When you buy your pot, make sure that it will be hardy in the frost. In areas where winter frosts are common, a non-frost-hardy pot will disintegrate into flaky shards of pottery.

◆ The compost – or, more correctly the soil 'medium' – that you put into the container for growing the rose is hugely important. Use a high-quality soil-based potting compost, such as John Innes No 3. This will give the right amount of stability, because it is heavier than a peat medium, and the fine hairs on the rose roots will anchor into it better than a looser medium, for example one comprising more organic material like peat.

◆ Apply peat as a surface mulch, to give the top layer an open, more 'airy' medium, and to give the pot an appearance of being 'finished off'.

◆ Water the pot regularly – this is likely to be daily in the summer – and make sure you feed the rose twice a year.

◆ Pot-grown roses are transportable, and they thrive best in full sun when they are in flower, and in a lightly shaded spot when the flowers fade. If you're clever with your gardening, when you move the roses, you could put other seasonal decorative containers in their place.

◆ Keeping a rose in the shade for nine or ten months of the year will weaken it over time. Unless you live on the equator, days are shorter in the winter than other times of year, so bring the pots back into the sun again during the winter.

ROSES AS HEDGING

Many rose varieties are suitable for growing as hedging, in fact they can make fabulous hedges and, depending on the type of rose, these can be suitable for large or small gardens. A hedge, of course, is where a line of plants are grown in which the individuality of each plant is lost. You will, therefore, need to choose varieties with a growth habit that enables them to meld their stems and branches seamlessly into those of their neighbour. Not all roses have this facility.

There are drawbacks to a rose hedge, and in some ways the more traditional hedging plants, such as conifers, privets and so on, are much better. The first drawback is that a rose hedge loses its leaves in winter, exposing your garden to the world – and the weather. Second, a rose hedge cannot be trimmed and kept to straight lines; the nature of the plants is that they are informal in style and uneven in shape. Third, no matter how hard you try, a rose hedge in shade will be a very poor and sparse hedge indeed and you cannot always choose to have a hedge in full sun. Roses, therefore, may not be the best choice for your hedging.

However, if you are able to overcome these drawbacks, a rose hedge will reward you by providing an almost unequalled and marvellous display of abundant flowers.

ABOVE *Rosa rugosa* 'Belle Poitevine' is one of the oldest and loveliest of the rugosa hybrids, and it makes an excellent hedge.

ABOVE *Rosa rugosa* 'Alba', first grown round 1800, is a white form of the wild rose – and ideal for hedging.

Picking the right variety is crucial: it should be hardy, repeat-flowering, abundantly supplied with leaves, and it should be as disease-resistant and as weather-tolerant as possible.

Forms of *Rosa rugosa* are the best of all for boundary hedges, but they can become large. The handsome leaves are mildew-proof, the prickly stems are animal- and intruder-proof, and most produce attractive hips that last from autumn and well into winter. I grew up with a long hedge of the variety 'Roseraie de l'Hay' AGM, and so have a particular soft spot for this rose.

However, there are many others from which to choose (see 'Shrub and Hedging Roses' on pages 138–47).

Maintaining a rose hedge is not difficult. Deadhead the flowers as soon as they fade, and prune the roses in winter. In dry summers water the hedge, and mulch it in spring with well-rotted manure or garden compost. To maintain the health of the plants, and to encourage plenty of flowers, feed in mid-spring and again in late spring with a proprietary rose fertilizer. And that should be just about all that you need to do.

GROWING ROSES INDOORS

These days you can take a trip to the garden centre and buy a small range of tiny roses to be used as pot plants for growing indoors. These are miniature varieties that have been raised in the nursery especially for indoor culture. They have a certain charm and bring a little taste of rose growing to those whose garden may be no more than a windowsill.

Indoor roses can be encouraged to flower several times throughout the year, starting in early spring. The secret is to ensure that the plants receive maximum light and adequate humidity. For maximum light, site the plant in a sunny window, but screen it from midday sun in summer. For the very best conditions, move the pot near to a fluorescent light at night in spring and autumn, but this is impractical for most of us.

For humidity, stand the pot on a 1in (2.5cm) layer of gravel in a waterproof tray. Keep the bottom of this layer wet at all times, but keep the water level below the top of the gravel, otherwise it could cause rotting of the roots that come into contact with it. Another efficient way to keep up humidity levels is to mist the leaves daily with a hand sprayer and clean water.

In theory you can condition these roses so that they can be grown outdoors, but usually this is met with limited success. The plants are seldom very hardy and invariably suffer from drying out unless kept in partial shade, but then they produce fewer flowers. If you do try to harden them up for the outside world, you should certainly transfer them to a more durable pot for outdoors, such as the terracotta types mentioned earlier.

Arguably, it is best to keep these roses simply as house plants. In fact the prices of these plants have come down so much since the first ones were produced in the 1980s, that they are almost best used as 'throw-away' plants after one season, much like bedding plants or the Christmas-flowering poinsettia pot plant.

ABOVE **Miniature roses, often unnamed varieties, are available for growing as house plants.**

TYPICAL PLANT HARDINESS ZONES FOR WESTERN EUROPE

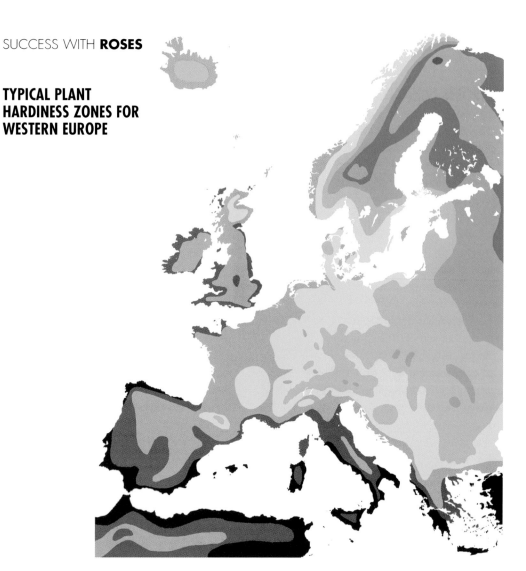

As mentioned in the Introduction on page 9, although roses are often labelled 'the flower of England', they are certainly not exclusive to England. Much breeding work takes place in the United Kingdom, United States, New Zealand and, indeed, most major countries, so it is easy to see that members of the *Rosa* genus are adaptable to a wide variety of climates.

Wherever you are – with the exception of the areas within the Arctic and Antarctic regions – you will be able to establish a rose garden. The usual restriction will be that of space, rather than one of climate. Gallicas, English roses and modern shrubs do well in what is called the 'Maritime' climate zone, which encompasses the British Isles. Hybrid tea roses, damasks and floribundas will do well here also, but are perhaps better in Mediterranean climates.

As sweeping generalizations go, species roses – particularly the rugosas – can survive in the USDA zones 3 and 4. At the other extreme, however, are the tropical and subtropical climate regions and, although roses can be grown here, the heat, humidity and dryness in the soil may require specific gardening aids, such as automated irrigation and spraying. Similarly, roses can be grown in some desert regions, provided there is adequate irrigation.

As you can see, roses are quite adaptable, and gardeners in most climate zones across the planet will find they are able to grow at least a few good plants.

TYPICAL PLANT HARDINESS ZONES FOR NORTH AMERICA

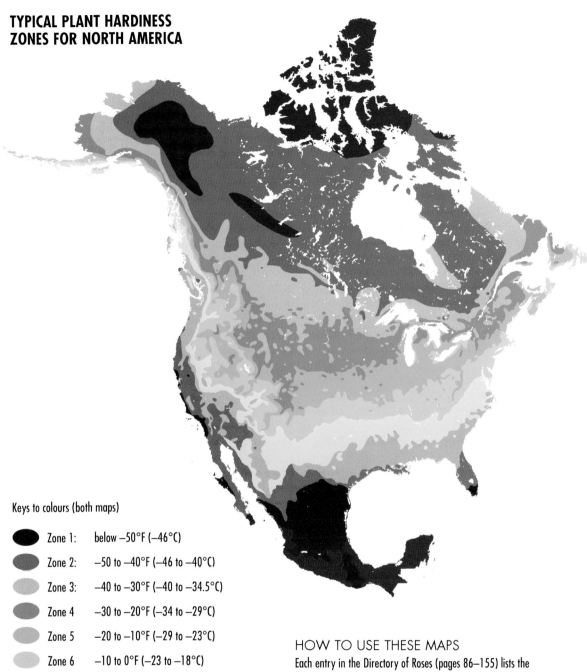

Keys to colours (both maps)

●	Zone 1:	below −50°F (−46°C)
●	Zone 2:	−50 to −40°F (−46 to −40°C)
●	Zone 3:	−40 to −30°F (−40 to −34.5°C)
●	Zone 4	−30 to −20°F (−34 to −29°C)
●	Zone 5	−20 to −10°F (−29 to −23°C)
●	Zone 6	−10 to 0°F (−23 to −18°C)
●	Zone 7	0 to 10°F (−18 to −12°C)
●	Zone 8	10 to 20°F (−12 to −7°C)
●	Zone 9	20 to 30°F (−7 to −1°C)
●	Zone 10	30 to 40°F (−1 to 4°C)
●	Zone 11	above 40°F (above 4°C)

HOW TO USE THESE MAPS

Each entry in the Directory of Roses (pages 86–155) lists the relevant zones where the plant can be grown successfully, based on these heat-zone maps. Find your location on the map and you can then identify the zone you belong to, though don't forget to take into account that cities are warmer than rural locations, and planting shelter belts of trees, or planting against a sunny wall and/or in raised, well-drained beds, can give plants better conditions in which to thrive.

CHAPTER 2

Designing your rose garden

Most of the world's large and famous rose gardens have huge areas devoted to swathes of rose beds, which look fantastic for the few months in the summer when roses are at their best. These gardens have been unashamedly created for rose enthusiasts, who are referred to in the fraternity as 'rosarians', but they frequently leave gardeners with other horticultural passions unexcited. And, when you take into consideration that, for at least nine months of the year, these rose gardens have little or no colour in them, you can begin to understand why roses are not universally liked and appreciated.

ABOVE 'Elmshorn' is a good shrub rose, particularly impressive when planted en masse.

In this book, however, my mission is to encourage those who have never attempted to grow roses seriously, and to provide incentives for them to do so, as well as providing a little more detail and insight into the subject for those who have dabbled previously in the rosarian arts. One of the best ways – if not the best way – is to discuss the subject of roses in design terms. Just how is it possible to incorporate rose plants into your garden so that: you gain maximum pleasure from them; they perform in their optimum way; your display of plants, and your clear proficiency in growing them, is seen as so rewarding to visiting neighbours, friends and family, that they, too, catch the rose 'bug'?

FLOWER BEDS

There are two types of flower bed – a planted area that is designed to be viewed from all sides (as distinct from a flower border, which is essentially viewed from one or more sides, but not the back). The first type of flower bed is the 'island bed', which usually has grass on all four sides, but gravel or paving surrounds are also common. The secret is to avoid having lots of smaller beds, and instead to concentrate on one or two big ones. You will notice the benefit of this particularly when cutting the grass, as it can be very tiresome to run the lawn mower up and down between lots of small beds.

Island beds are usually 'formal', with straight or rounded sides. With these, it is more effective to plant the roses in a strictly geometric pattern. Hybrid teas and floribundas are most suited to this type of setting, but it is not a good idea to mix them together. Hybrid teas can be used where the bed is closer to the house, and where the blooms demand to be viewed close up. Floribundas are the best choice where a large splash of long-lasting colour is desired.

Occasional standard roses of the same or a contrasting colour can be used to add a touch of height to the scene. However, the most important requirement is to keep things in proportion, so remember that small bushes are suited to small beds.

The second type of flower bed is often referred to as a 'flanking bed'. Here, the bed is used to divide the lawn from, say, a pathway or driveway. They are frequently narrower and longer than island beds, and it is not uncommon to see a single line of bush roses being used. Again, it is important to provide height, and standard or weeping standard roses can be planted at strategic places.

It is practical to keep the depth of your rose bed to 5ft (1.5m) or less, otherwise at pruning and deadheading time you will have to get right onto the bed and tread between the plants – and the thorns can be painful.

ABOVE **Rose gardens that are dedicated purely to roses can be dull at 'quiet' times of the year.**

ABOVE **Roses are perfect additions to gardens which have mixed planting schemes.**

FLOWER BORDERS

Most gardens these days have flower borders rather than flower beds, and they are nearly always sited along the edge and back of a garden. The same rules about the planting of roses apply, apart from the fact that the tallest varieties should be planted at the back of the border, and the shortest at the front.

It is more usual to see an 'informal' border, with curved edges, and with plants grouped and spaced according to their height and spread. Because there is frequently going to be a back wall or fence, you can use climbing roses and ramblers as well.

A deep border of 10ft (3m) or so can have blocks of roses and will sustain some four or five roses deep, from front to back; a medium border with a depth of around 6ft (2m) will be able to accommodate two staggered rows; and a narrow border of just 3ft (1m) or so will only be able to house a single row. Unlike the dedicated rose beds, here you can plant staggered and grouped plants to create drifts of colour.

ABOVE This rose border is formal (with straight edges), but most domestic gardens are more attractive if the edges are curved, or 'informal'.

INTEGRATION

Arguably the best way to display roses in modern gardens is to associate them with other plants. Few of us, in any case, have the luxury of space in our gardens to create even mini-versions of the great rose gardens with dedicated rose beds, so it is much more practical – and more pleasing to the eye throughout the year – to integrate roses with other plants. This means, of course, that in the final reckoning you will not be able to grow nearly as many roses. But what plants make good 'companions' for roses?

Most shrub roses grow well with other flowering or wall shrubs. Try integrating the summer-flowering climber *Rosa filipes* 'Kiftsgate' AGM with golden-leaved hops. The combination of white rose flowers and yellow hop foliage is stunning. Try also spring-flowering forsythia and Japanese quince (*Chaenomeles*), which bloom in advance of roses, or the summer-flowering Californian lilac (*Ceanothus*), which looks particularly delightful with white roses.

Clematis certainly make good partners with roses, as their cultural needs are similar: they both grow best in well-drained, moist, fertile soil with added feed a couple of times a year.

Clematis can be very effective when grown 'through' – that is, supported by – a climbing rose. With careful choice the clematis will bloom just before or just after the rose, which means that you will get double the flowering time, with different colours and flower shapes, from the same space.

Or, to be extravagant, you could opt to have both plants flowering at the same time for a very powerful display. A blue clematis such as 'Perle d'Azur' and a white rose – such as 'White Cockade' or 'Climbing Iceberg' – look wonderful together.

I've seen a garden where the owner had created a border of orange-flowered lilies (*Lilium pardalinum*) with the strong-growing yellow shrub rose 'Golden Wings' AGM, and the effect was breathtaking.

ABOVE *Rosa filipes* 'Kiftsgate' AGM, although vigorous, grows well with other plants, including the golden-leaved hop.

UNDERPLANTING

You should never overlook the underplanting, either. The principle aims of growing other plants below and around roses are to make use of the empty ground, to extend the season of interest, and also to show off the roses to best advantage. Usually gardeners grow fairly low-growing annual bedding plants, such as pansies in the spring and begonias in the summer.

This does involve quite a bit of work, planting in between the thorny and sometimes vicious roses, and it may cause some disturbance to the rose plants and roots. Perhaps it is better, therefore, to grow annuals around the edges of the rose bed or flower border, and to grow low-growing perennials – that do not require annual planting – between the roses. Try the silvery lamb's tongue (*Stachys lanata*), the silvery-grey hummocks of old-fashioned pinks, or the silvery blue-leaved rue (*Ruta graveolens*).

One of the most stunning combinations of rose underplanting I've seen was of the deep pink-purple 'Madame Isaac Pereire' AGM, underplanted with a solid carpet of perennial summer-flowering violets. I can only imagine the effect of a similar underplanting with a yellow rose (such as the English rose 'Graham Thomas'), a white rose (such as 'Madame Alfred Carrière' AGM), or a pale pink rose (such as 'Céleste').

Finally, if you are attracted to the idea of a pure rose bed, it is possible to avoid a long and barren period in winter and early spring by planting spring bulbs, followed by forget-me-nots between the roses. These will serve to mask the rose stems until the first buds open, and neither bulbs nor forget-me-nots will rob too many soil nutrients from the roses. Remember, however, that these plants will die back and need to be be cleared.

ABOVE **Garden sculpture and underplanting add a modern twist to a traditional border.**

THE COLOUR DILEMMA

Of course, if you mix roses with other plants, you will be creating a variety of heights, habits, leaf forms and flower colours within your bed or border. But if you do fancy growing roses together en masse, you should be careful when it comes to colour. The large public rose gardens referred to at the start of this chapter generally feature only one variety of rose per bed, and this is the traditional way – if the garden is big enough. In most gardens today this is not practical, and in any case could lead to dull patches at certain times of year. However, it is also important to avoid the other extreme – a large bed filled with single plants of many different varieties, which would give the 'fruit-salad' effect. The best plan is to use three to five bushes of each variety per bed, or area of the border.

In terms of colour choice, you can obtain all sorts of advice from the experts about which colours harmonize and which do not, but grouping colours is a matter of personal taste, and you should not worry too much about clashes. It is, however, best to avoid planting different reds together, as they can be the worst kind of clashing: separate them by planting white, pale yellow or cream varieties as dividers between them.

ABOVE **A modern rose garden, with a single colour theme and decorative water feature.**

POSITIONING FOR SCENT

Ask a non-gardener to name a feature of the rose, and they will almost certainly say fragrance. These plants are, of course, a mainstay of the perfume industry – artificially emulating the flower fragrance has been the target of every perfumer since early times – and the scent must play an important role in our own home gardens, too.

While there are some roses that have a more powerful fragrance than others, it should not be forgotten that the strength of a scent can vary markedly from day to day – or even during the course of a single day, depending on temperature and humidity – and the age of the flower: some roses possess the most powerful scent just as the buds have opened, while others are stronger just before the flower dies. Individual people vary, too, in the amount of fragrance they can detect.

Grow scented roses where you are most likely to appreciate them. Planting them next to, or around, house doors and windows is obvious. You should also plant them around the periphery of patios or sitting areas, and pathways. It is a good idea to grow scented roses in containers, as these can be moved to strategically important places when the plants are in bloom.

Some of the most strongly scented roses include 'Ernest H. Morse', 'Fragrant Cloud' and 'Whisky Mac' (hybrid teas); 'Iceberg', 'Korresia' and 'Southampton' AGM (floribundas); and 'Albertine', 'New Dawn' AGM and 'Wedding Day' (climbers).

Roses with aromatic foliage that gives off a spicy fragrance are most appealing too. There is *Rosa primula*, which has an extraordinary aroma reminiscent of incense, most powerful during heavy, thundery weather. Then there is *Rosa serafinii*, a small, twiggy bush bearing white flowers in summer and small red hips in autumn. If you pinch the leaves a sweet, almost chocolate-like scent comes from them.

If it is happy where it is, the sweet briar (*Rosa eglanteria*), native to the UK, will self-sow. If you are fortunate and this happens in your garden, prune out all its flowered stems each winter, to encourage the production of young shoots that keep on growing right through into autumn. The young foliage gives off a delicious smell of stewing apples.

The rugosa roses are grown for their sweetly scented flowers and frequently for their bright autumn fruits. But they also have appealing, rough-textured foliage with a spicy scent when crushed.

ABOVE **Fragrant roses should be planted next to pathways, or sitting areas, where they can be enjoyed at close quarters.**

CLIMBERS AND SUPPORTS

In my view, a garden without a climbing or rambler rose to clothe its higher parts with colour is a poor garden. But with these plants, the method of support used plays a major part in determining the success of the display. On a fence or wall, a climbing rose should be trained along horizontal galvanized steel wires strung tightly between bolts, or 'vine eyes', which are driven into the woodwork, or the mortar in brickwork. The wires should be suspended about 3in (7.5cm) from the wall or fence, to allow a reasonable circulation of air around the stems.

If neither the house wall nor the garden-boundary wall or fence are suitable for growing roses, opt for one of the following: arches, pergolas, pillars, or catenaries (heavy-duty ropes

ABOVE **Climbing roses can be used to clothe boring vertical surfaces or, as here, to enhance a decorative woven structure.**

ABOVE 'American Pillar' is a medium-sized rambler. The vivid red-pink flowers have white centres.

slung between upright posts, which roses are trained along). The best roses for training up these, without doubt, are the ramblers – their canes are far more flexible than those of climbers, and so it is easier to direct them where you wish them to go. They will make a stunning display, but sadly for only six or seven weeks in summer. For some gardeners this will be sufficient, but if you want later flowers, you should choose 'remontant' (simply repeat-flowering, or often called 'recurrent') climbers. Their canes will be stiffer, but you should not have too many problems if you train in the canes early enough, when they are much more pliable.

Both pergolas and catenaries are supported by pillars, against which the roses should be planted. Here, the shoots should be spiralled round the pillars.

If your climbers and ramblers are slow to make progress at first, do not worry. It is quite usual for them to take perhaps three years to become established, after which they will romp away.

ABOVE Catenaries are traditional structures for supporting rambling roses; heavy-duty ropes are slung between upright posts.

VICTORIAN ROSE WALK

If you are fanatically enthusiastic about roses and you have sufficient space to create a garden dedicated to them, you could consider a Victorian rose walk. This is a popular alternative to simple rose beds which was, not surprisingly, first seen during Victorian times.

A typical 'walk' will have six or seven different types of rose, with three or four varieties or classic rose shapes for each type: some will flower once in summer, while others will be remontant, giving a longer display.

Traditionally the beds would be some 20ft (6m) long and about 4ft (1.2m) wide. Before planting, the 'walk' would be marked out so that the beds are clearly indicated. The individual plants were positioned so that each shrub rose was approximately 5ft (1.5m) from its neighbour. Standard roses would be planted within the gaps left between the shrubs.

To give height, there would also be some climbing or rambling roses growing on upright structures (such as trellises or pillars); these could be sited at the ends or backs of the beds, or at an end wall. In fact, it would not be unusual for the central pathway to end at a wall, and traditionally there may be a piece of statuary or other object there to create a focal point. The roses would reach their mature dimensions in about three to four years.

It is fun to choose modern-day roses, and there are plenty to choose from, but to make your rose walk more authentic you could choose plants of nineteenth-century origin. Those to consider would include shrub roses such as 'Fantin-Latour', 'Königin von Dänemark', 'Madame Hardy' and 'Cécile Brunner', standards such as 'Boule de Neige', and also ramblers such as 'Albéric Barbier' AGM.

ABOVE **This modern interpretation of a Victorian rose 'walk' has a waterway where the path would have been.**

CHAPTER 3

Buying and planting roses

Once you have decided where you would like to plant roses, and you have identified suitable and desirable rose varieties (the Directory of Roses on pages 86–155 will help), you will need to buy the plants. This is not as simple as it sounds, and it can be fraught with issues, depending on where you go, and what you want. Essentially, roses are sold in two main forms: the modern style of container-grown types, and the older and more traditional bare-root type.

CONTAINER-GROWN ROSES

Container-grown roses are sold at every garden centre, and they do have many advantages over bare-root roses, which are described on the facing page. The first is that they can be planted right through the summer months as well as in the winter. Remember, however, that planting anything during hot weather — not just roses — means that you must pay particular attention to watering. New plants that have not become established in the soil will quickly die if not watered after a few days of hot weather.

When choosing containerized roses do not be swayed by a fabulous display of flowers; look 'through' these to examine the state of the plant itself and make sure its stems are healthy and strong, with no damage or disease.

ABOVE Container-grown roses will always have a name label — check these to make sure you are buying the correct variety.

LEFT Good-quality climber or rambler roses should have two or more stems, each at least 18in (45cm) long.

Try and ensure also that the roses are genuine container-grown plants, not bare-root specimens that have recently been potted up, perhaps hurriedly, for the nursery or garden centre to make a quick sale and get rid of them. You can tell if roses have been in their containers for the proper length of time by moss or algae on the soil surface, although an excess of this can also indicate slapdash and undesirable practices in the nursery, where plant hygiene – that is, weeding and control of pests and diseases – have been less than rigorous.

Another way to identify how long a rose has been in a pot is to see if the roots are beginning to push through the holes in the base of the container. Most importantly, however, you should ask; if you go to a reliable nursery the staff there should be able to give you accurate information.

BARE-ROOT ROSES

'Bare-root' roses are those that have been grown in the nursery fields and are then lifted during the dormant season for selling. Most of these are destined for sale in smaller plant nurseries, the thriving mail-order rose business and in stores and supermarkets. In the case of the latter two, these bare-root roses are pre-packed and sealed, usually with some moisture kept around the roots, by packing in moist tissue paper or a small amount of compost.

If you really know what you are looking for, it is possible to buy excellent plants in this way, and they are usually cheaper than container-grown types because you are not buying the pot and soil. You also have the advantage of seeing if the plant has a well-developed root system. Beware, however, of those with wrinkled, dried-up stems, or premature growth caused by high temperatures in transit or in the shop, where the transparent packaging has created a mini 'greenhouse' around the plants.

The presence of shoots and/or leaves can also be a very good indication of the length of time the rose has been packed, and out of the ground. The hot atmosphere of a shop itself is rarely ideal – which is why cut-flower florists are usually very cool places – and so it is sensible to buy any such bare-root roses within just a few days of them appearing on the shelves.

Also, beware of specimens with spindly little shoots, or any that are discoloured with disease. Saleable plants should have a good, fibrous root system and a minimum of two strong, firm shoots, no thinner than a pencil and preferably thicker. Standard roses should be double-budded; that is, they should have two points of origin for the 'head' of shoots at the top of the main stem.

Although bare-root roses are available for much of the year, late autumn is the ideal time for planting them, and this is when there will be ample stocks in nurseries and garden centres.

ABOVE **Bare-root roses are often sold in cardboard sleeves and have their roots packed in moist tissue paper, or a small amount of peat.**

MAIL- AND INTERNET-ORDER ROSES

Many gardeners prefer to choose roses from a mail-order catalogue. The main advantages of this method are that you can frequently find new, rare, or unusual varieties; you don't need to leave the comfort of your armchair to order your selection – apart from going out to post your letter – and very often the roses will be cheaper than they would be from retail outlets.

The disadvantages to mail-order purchasing of plants – not just roses – is that the colour reproduction in the catalogue may be some way off from the accurate colouring of the flowers, also, most importantly, you do not see the quality of the plants before you part with your money. However, most bona-fide nurseries offering a mail-order service will want their reputation to remain intact, so they should be happy to replace plants – or refund you – provided you complain as soon as the plants arrive, and you do not leave the plants for days or weeks before you make your claim.

These days the Internet is a variation of the mail-order business. The bigger rose nurseries will usually list the roses they stock and show pictures in the 'catalogue' section of their websites. This is a much more immediate way to buy your plants – requiring you to use a credit or debit card to secure your purchases – but you are vulnerable to the same mail-order disadvantages as those listed above.

ABOVE **Buying roses via Internet websites is becoming more and more popular, but you do not get to see the actual plants that you are buying.**

VIEWING ROSES IN GARDENS

There is no doubt at all that the best way to choose roses is to see them growing in a garden, preferably in your local area and, if possible, over a full season. You will then be able to assess any defects, as well as noting the size of the plants and/or flowers, so you can work out your own spacings in your garden. This is not something you can tell from seeing young specimens in containers in shops, or on the Internet.

ABOVE **The best way to choose roses is to visit a garden where they are named — and when they are in full bloom.**

WHAT TO LOOK FOR WHEN BUYING

A good-quality rose — whether miniature and patio, or the bush or shrub varieties — should normally have between three and five stems, each neatly pruned back by the nursery to between 10 and 18in (25 and 45cm) in length. They should be well and uniformly furnished with main and fibrous roots.

Climbers and ramblers should have two or more stems, each at least 18in (45cm) long. The stems should be green and clean, and buds should be dormant. Long, pale green, or white shoots from the stems should not be present.

Avoid any roses that appear to have suckers, which weaken the whole plant, and any plant that is lop-sided, with roots concentrated on one side only. Avoid container-grown roses where the compost level is far above or below the graft point (or 'union') at the stem base. There are far too many container roses that appear as if on stilts, with the compost washed away from the roots.

Finally, as with any container-grown plants, there should be minimal amounts of moss or weed growth on the compost itself.

CENTRE **Good-quality bush roses should normally have three to five stems.**

RIGHT **There should be minimal amounts of weed and moss growth on the compost surface.**

SOIL AND SITUATION

Contrary to popular belief, roses do not prefer a clay soil – they can do very well indeed on a sandy soil. The important thing is that the soil needs to be free-draining, and must be moisture-retentive. This sounds like a contradiction, but in fact most soils do have both these qualities.

If your soil is extremely sandy, and does not hold water well, you must incorporate plenty of humus into it before planting. This can be provided in the form of well-rotted garden compost or animal manure, which should be mixed well into the soil around and within the planting hole. However, do not plant a rose right into this material, as it is too strong for the fine root hairs and will burn them, so make sure that the compost or manure is mixed with the garden soil.

Similarly, if your soil is heavy clay, and water sits in muddy puddles on the surface instead of penetrating it, again your roses will not appreciate this. So bulky organic matter as described should be used in this instance to break up the soil, to aid drainage, and to provide valuable nutrition to what is likely to be an impoverished soil.

Roses are at their absolute best in the sun, and will only do really well if they have it for most of the day.

ABOVE **Home-made garden compost, as long as it is well-rotted, should be incorporated into the soil before planting.**

SOIL PREPARATION

When you are creating a completely new rose bed, some digging is required, for your roses may be in their new home for a long time – perhaps 15 or more years – and it is only sensible to give them the best start possible. 'Single digging' should be sufficient, unless your soil is exceptionally heavy and badly drained, or the new bed is being dug out of a compacted turf area, in which case 'double digging' will be required (see facing page).

ABOVE **After single or double digging, it is important to firm and rake the soil level prior to planting.**

SINGLE DIGGING METHOD

1 Dig a trench the length of the bed – or at least the area designated for the roses – to about the width and depth of the spade's blade. Remove weeds as you go, and dig out completely any pieces of perennial weed roots that you find.

2 Place the soil from this trench in a wheelbarrow. Transport it to the far end of the area to be dug, and then return to the trench.

3 Break up the subsoil in the base of the trench with a fork, remove any further weed roots and incorporate plenty of organic material, as described above.

4 Dig a second trench alongside the first one, and fill the first trench with the turned soil – known as 'spoil'.

5 Continue the procedure across the area, in progressive trenches, until you come to the end. The last trench should be filled with the soil from the first trench (i.e. the soil that had been transported via the wheelbarrow).

Where tests indicate that a heavy clay soil is deficient in lime, a dressing of hydrated lime will help to improve its structure. Gypsum (or calcium sulphate) is sometimes used for this purpose, at rates up to 2lb per yd^2 (900g per 0.84m^2), as this amount will not alter the alkalinity of the soil.

DOUBLE DIGGING METHOD

1 Dig a trench some 18in (45cm) wide and 12in (30cm) deep at one side of the bed or border, placing the soil in a wheelbarrow or to one side.

2 Next, fork over the bottom of the trench to the full depth of the fork's prongs, working in bulky organic matter.

3 Dig another trench alongside the first, transferring the soil from the new trench into the first trench.

4 Fork over the bottom of the second trench, then dig a third alongside and repeat the process, working your way across the bed until you get to the last trench, which can be filled in with the soil pile from the first trench.

CHALKY SOILS

If you live in a high-chalk area where, say, there is a maximum topsoil layer of 18in (45cm) or so before you get to the chalk layer, you will have difficulty in growing roses. You could opt to grow only the lime-tolerant types, mainly the alba, damask and hybrid musk shrub roses, or you could import a 2ft (60cm) depth of new, suitable topsoil. Alternatively, with your normal soil you could dig a much bigger planting hole, some 2ft (60cm) or deeper, and incorporate a generous quantity of tree and shrub planting mixture (bagged loam and organic material, available from garden retailers).

CHANGING THE SOIL

If you are planting new roses into a bed in which roses have grown for a long time, the soil is likely to be 'rose-sick'. Due to a build-up of soil parasites and a depletion of mineral reserves, newly planted roses may not do at all well, even if the previous plants have appeared reasonably healthy.

The answer is to change the top 12–15in (30–38cm) of soil, or to sterilize it chemically. You may even opt to plant the roses elsewhere, using the previous rose bed for other plants instead.

To change the soil, dig out the top layer, to the depth stated, and exchange it with soil from, say, the vegetable garden or an empty border. Or, if you have the capacity within your garden to accommodate extra volume, buy in some new, clean topsoil from a supplier. Before replacing the fresh soil in the rose bed, dig over the bottom and empty in a good layer of rotted organic matter. Allow the replaced soil to settle naturally during the winter before planting.

To sterilize the soil, dig the bed over to a depth of 12in (30cm) in early autumn, while the soil is still fairly warm, adding a good layer of well-rotted organic matter. Apply a soil sterilant at the maker's recommended dosage, then cover the area with polythene for four or five weeks to retain the fumes and allow them time to act in the soil.

DRESSING THE SOIL

Immediately before you set the plants in the ground, apply a dressing of bonemeal fertilizer over the area at the rate of 2oz per yd^2 (65g per m^2). Work it into the surface of the soil, using a hoe or rake, tread the area firm and then rake it level.

ABOVE Roses should be fed with bonemeal fertilizer at the rate of 2oz per yd^2 (65g per m^2).

PLANT PREPARATION

Just before you put a rose into its hole, there are certain things you should do to give it the best start:

1 If any of the stems or roots appears to be shrivelled, submerge the whole plant in water for several hours. Roots, particularly, should never be allowed to become dry – keep them covered at all times whilst the rose is out of the soil.

2 When the plant is sufficiently hydrated, cut off any leaves, hips or flower buds, which may still be present, as well as any really thin or decayed shoots. Cut back, also, any damaged or very long roots, to about 12in (30cm).

Sometimes experts advocate cutting a rose back to just a few buds, in other words quite a severe pruning, at the time of planting. And whether this is carried out whilst the plant is still in your hands, or when it has been firmed in place, is a matter of choice. Personally I do not tend to prune as severely at planting; instead I cut the stems back by half, or so, and allow them to settle in. I will make sure, however, that from the normal pruning time – late winter – I prune them thoroughly.

RIGHT **If stems or roots appear to be shrivelled, submerge the whole of the plant in water for several hours.**

43

ABOVE **If bare-root roses arrive before you are ready to plant them, 'heel' them in — covering the roots, to prevent them from drying out.**

ABOVE **Dig a hole — it should be approximately twice the size of the roots to accommodate them comfortably.**

ABOVE **Incorporate some shop-bought or home-made planting mixture into the dug hole.**

PLANTING BARE-ROOT BUSH ROSES

Mid-autumn is the best time for planting, as the roses have time to settle in before the soil becomes too cold for root growth, and they will make a quicker start in the spring. But roses can be planted at any time when they are dormant, or nearly so, from late autumn to early spring, providing you do not choose a frosty spell and the ground is not waterlogged. Autumn planting gets the job out of the way when there is probably not quite so much to do in the garden.

Plants ordered in mid-summer, or at other times, will probably be arriving now anyway. Unpack them as soon as you receive them, and heel them in so that the roots do not dry out. To do this, dig a trench and place the bushes in it, close together, with the soil just above the graft union, until you are ready to plant them out. Aim to plant them as soon as possible, but they should remain alive and reasonably healthy until mid-winter. If you leave them longer than this, the plants will grow new roots into the soil around them, and this should be avoided.

If plants arrive when the ground is frozen, put them temporarily in a frost-free shed, and cover them with sacking or straw.

Although planting a rose is a single-person job, two hands never seem to be enough:

ABOVE **The 'union' is the point where the rose was budded onto the rootstock.**

a third would be absolutely perfect, just to hold the plant in place while you're doing everything else around it!

So, now to the planting: start by digging the hole. The soil from it should be mixed with a shop-bought planting mixture, or you can make your own by mixing it with peat or peat-substitute, and a handful of slow-release fertilizer. This mixture should be kept in a pile next to the hole.

The hole itself should be deep enough for the budding union of the rose (that is, the point where the plant was budded on to the rootstock) to be about 1in (2.5cm) below soil level, and wide enough for the roots to fan out as evenly as possible all round, if they grow that way. Many roses have all their roots pointing in one direction and these should be placed at one side of the planting hole, not in the middle, and the roots then spread out as widely as possible.

Hold the rose in position, replace the planting mixture over the roots, and gently shake the plant so that the mixture falls down between the roots. Fill with more of the mixture, and then tread firmly, but not too hard, around the roots without damaging them. Replace all the soil, firm with your foot again, and level the area off. Finally, apply at least one – and preferably two – watering cans of water to help the roots establish.

ABOVE **Apply at least one – and preferably two – cans of water to help the roots to establish.**

ABOVE **Secure the rose in position by treading firmly around the roots – but not too hard, to avoid damaging them.**

ABOVE **Hold the rose in position and replace the soil and planting mixture over the roots – this should be set just below soil level .**

PLANTING CONTAINER-GROWN BUSH ROSES

These can be planted at any time of year but, if you are planting during the summer, or a period of hot weather in spring or autumn, you must check for watering almost on a daily basis, until such time as the general soil is consistently moist.

Just because container-grown roses have a neat root-ball when removed from the pot, do not be fooled into thinking that you simply need to dig a hole the same size as the root-ball, and then drop it in. If you did this on a heavy clay soil you would inadvertently create a sump from which water would be slow to drain, and this could cause the rose roots to rot.

It is a good idea, therefore, to break up the surrounding soil and the base of the hole at planting time, and then to use the planting mixture (as described on the previous page) to fill in around the root-ball. Firm the rose in position, and water it in.

PLANTING CLIMBERS

When setting a climber or rambler rose against a wall, you may have to plant it 12in (30cm) or so away from the wall, in order to avoid the footings: make the hole and position the rose at an angle, with the top growth pointing towards the wall. Point the roots away from the wall, where the soil will often be dry, towards more moist soil. Water the rose in, and check it regularly for the first year, particularly during hot weather.

ABOVE **Dig a hole and break up the surrounding soil. You can use a straight piece of wood to check whether the hole is deep enough.**

ABOVE **Firm the rose in position, and then water in.**

ABOVE **To flourish, climbing roses like these should be planted some 12in (30cm) away from the support structure, to avoid the footings.**

PLANTING STANDARD ROSES

These need a relatively shallow hole, just enough for the roots to be covered. If they are more deeply planted, the rootstocks, which are usually taken from *Rosa rugosa*, will sucker freely.

A stake should always support a standard rose, and it should be driven into the hole before planting, so as to avoid damaging the plant's roots. The top of the stake should come up just to the budding union, which in standards is only slightly beneath the head of branches.

PLANTING DISTANCES

It is important to allow the correct spacings between roses when you plant them, otherwise they will soon encroach upon each other, resulting in poorer plants and fewer flowers, which will become a nightmare to manage. Here are the recommended distances between plants:

Hybrid tea 18in (45cm)

Floribundas 27in (68cm)

Miniatures 9–12in (23–30cm), depending on their eventual size

Shrub roses 4–5ft (1.2–1.5m), depending on their eventual size

It is impossible to give precise planting distances for all other types of rose as they vary so greatly at maturity. With these, you will need to exercise caution and common sense, and always be prepared to re-site roses at the correct time if they grow too big, or encroach on other plants.

ABOVE **Always stake standard roses so that the stake top finishes just beneath the head of the branches, as shown here.**

CHAPTER 4

Pruning roses

Even beginner gardeners know that, regardless of what other plants they might be growing, it is the roses that will, at some stage, need pruning. Without an annual trim, roses will soon become lanky and unsightly, with just a few miserable flowers.

Although we will be showing you here how to prune bush roses in the orthodox way, there is an increasing school of thought that suggests these plants flourish just as well if they are cut back in a haphazard way – say with a hedge trimmer. Certainly, evidence now suggests that it is neither essential to cut to a bud and ensure that the cut is not too close, nor to ensure that the slope of cut is not too flat or steep.

The decision as to which way to prune is of course yours, but at least, if you wish to do it in the old-fashioned way, all of the information you need is published here.

ABOVE The old skills, of carefully pruning roses to an outward-facing bud, have been questioned in recent years.

ABOVE 'Blue Peter' is a delightful miniature bush rose, but it requires pruning every winter in order to remain compact.

FIVE REASONS TO PRUNE

Why do we prune plants at all? The reason for this systematic cutting back of all woody plants – not just roses – can be summed up as follows:

1 To maintain the desired shape and habit.

2 To keep the plant to a desired size.

3 To remove dead, weak, unhealthy and overcrowded growth.

4 To improve flowering and fruiting.

5 To improve foliage and stems.

So, let's look at each in turn.

SHAPE AND HABIT

Most trees and shrubs look their best when they are allowed to grow naturally and, in a natural setting, it is best to retain a plant's natural shape whenever possible.

Roses, with their somewhat haphazard and spiky growths may be regarded as an exception, but they do have defined shapes, and to allow them to grow awkwardly takes away much of their charm.

Awkwardly placed shoots will upset the balance occasionally, and such growths should be cut out. When one part of a plant is more vigorous than another, causing the overall appearance of the plant to be unbalanced, remember the general pruning principle that the strong shoots should be lightly pruned, while the weaker shoots need hard pruning. This is because hard pruning stimulates vigorous growth, so cutting back strong growths will merely encourage more vigorous shoots to be produced, which will accentuate the unbalanced shape further. Similarly, hard pruning will stimulate the weaker shoots into putting on considerably more growth.

RE-SHAPING ROSES

Rose plants that have grown out of balance can be re-shaped following these general guidelines:

METHOD

1 Remove straggling branches to a shoot or bud within the main bulk of the plant.

2 Carefully but systematically reduce the number of growths on the 'good' side of the plant – that is, the side with the most growth.

3 Cut back weak shoots hard, and strong shoots lightly on the 'bad' side of the plant.

4 Feed the plant with a good general fertilizer.

5 Mulch with well-rotted compost or manure.

ABOVE 'Dublin Bay' is a climber that is ideal for growing on a pillar, but it also performs very well as a shrub or hedging rose.

ABOVE The old centifolia shrub rose 'Fantin-Latour' AGM produces delicately scented blooms of clear, deep pink.

KEEPING PLANTS TO SIZE

Because of the pressures of space and modern living, most of us are faced with smaller gardens than our ancestors enjoyed. It has, therefore, become essential either to select and grow plants that will achieve a modest size when fully developed, or to ensure that we limit the size of larger plants by keeping them under control. In other words, we should prune them carefully so that they do not grow too big for the space allocated to them.

Bush and shrub roses, in the main, do not outgrow their allotted spaces, although without pruning they will become uncomfortably large, but it is certainly the case that climbing and rambler roses can produce long, whippy, growths that can soon encroach upon a pathway, or grow into neighbouring plants.

Similarly, rose hedges – if left to their own devices – will encroach upon the bordering lawn or pathway. Remember, too, that roses have thorns, and if your plants – hedge or otherwise – are flowing over onto a public walkway, you may have to suffer the wrath of passers-by with damaged clothing or scratches.

ABOVE 'Angela Rippon' is a salmon-pink miniature bush rose, ideal for growing in containers.

CUTTING OUT UNWANTED GROWTH

Roses that are not maintained – that is, pruned regularly or at the very least annually – can often become a dense mass of tangled branches, with the result that the shoots in the middle of the mass are deprived of light and air and prone to dying back. During windy weather the stems can rub together, causing injury to themselves and the branches they are rubbing against. All of these conditions lead to a greatly increased risk of disease.

It is frequently necessary, therefore, to 'open out' the plants to enable sunshine and air to reach every branch and shoot, so ripening the wood and swelling the buds. It is always advisable to remove unhealthy growth, as well as those shoots that are straggly and misshapen. Dead, diseased and pest-ridden wood should be cut away, back to clean, healthy wood. The diseased prunings should then be burnt before the problems have time to spread to any susceptible neighbours.

Weak and feeble shoots are unlikely to produce many flowers or the ensuing hips (which in some varieties can be the reason for growing them), and their removal will facilitate ripening of the remaining wood.

ABOVE **This rambler rose is growing up and through the remains of an old tree trunk – it will need pruning after flowering.**

ABOVE **Some roses are prone to making long, whippy shoots. If these are not cut back in autumn the rose could suffer 'wind-rock'.**

IMPROVE FLOWERING AND FRUITING

Decoration is what gardening is all about, and we would be failing as gardeners were we to allow our roses to produce less than their optimum decorative effect. In the case of roses, achieving optimum flowering is largely to do with timing.

There are several schools of thought where the pruning of bush roses is concerned. They should certainly be pruned while they are dormant – between late autumn and early spring – and, if you live in a cooler climate, the later you leave it the better. Some gardeners advocate the complete pruning in autumn, but this can run the risk of winter frosts attacking young, tender, premature growths. Others prefer to just tip the roses back in autumn – to prevent autumn and winter winds rocking and loosening the tall plants in the soil – and save the main pruning until late winter. Neither option is right nor wrong and the eventual decision is a matter of personal preference.

It generally follows that flowers will, ultimately, lead to fruit. So, if you are wanting to maximize a rose's potential for hip production, more or less the same pruning guidelines apply as for flowering plants: continually aim to encourage productive growth.

ABOVE **It is important to tie in the stems of climber roses regularly, as loose stems cannot easily be bent backwards when they are long.**

IMPROVE FOLIAGE AND STEMS

The importance of 'quality' leaves and stems in roses is secondary to the flowering, but they do still need to be healthy and look attractive. The rule of thumb with roses is that leaves are produced only on the current season's growth. Therefore the more vigorous this growth is, the larger and more profuse the foliage will be. Also, in a few rare instances there are roses with variegated leaves, and pruning (combined with a feeding programme) will help to accentuate the tones.

ABOVE **'Freedom' AGM is a hybrid tea rose with freely produced double blooms of bright yellow.**

MAKING CUTS

The most important rule when it comes to making a pruning cut is that the pruned stem must always terminate with a bud, where buds are visible. Additionally, the cut must be as reasonably close to the bud as possible without damaging it.

When secateurs are used, the blades should be placed just above the bud. With a pruning knife, however, the cut should start on the side opposite to the bud, at approximately the same level. The knife is then drawn towards the bud, but in a direction slanting upwards, so that the shoot is severed slightly above it.

If a cut is made between two buds, but the tip of the pruned shoot is a long distance from the bud below it, there is nothing to draw the sap up the shoot, so it will gradually die back. One is then left with a 'snag' – the gardener's term for a dead piece of wood resulting from incorrect pruning.

Snags are frequently seen in the fork of two closely growing shoots, where the person pruning has not taken the trouble to remove the centre piece of wood cleanly. A useful tool here is a joiner's padsaw, which has a very narrow blade.

In an ideal situation you should be cutting to a bud that is pointing in the right direction. It is important to keep the centre of the rose as 'open' as possible, in order that the sun can ripen wood in the inner parts of the plant, and also that air can circulate freely here. Therefore, when pruning, wherever possible prune to a bud that is facing 'outwards' from the centre of the plant.

The angle (or slope) of the cut is important, as this helps rainwater to run off the surface. You should not, however, make the angle of cut so oblique as to expose an excessive surface area for the entry of frost or disease.

COMMON FAULTS WHEN PRUNING STEMS (AND ONE CORRECT CUT)

a making the cut too far from the bud
b making the cut too close to the bud
c sloping away from the bud at too sharp an angle
d sloping towards the bud
e a torn or ragged cut will not heal effectively, so will allow the entry of pests and diseases
f correctly pruned

PRUNING BUSH ROSES

When to prune bush roses is a matter of some debate (see page 52), but they should certainly be pruned when they are dormant, which means between late autumn and early spring.

HYBRID TEAS

The aim when pruning is to encourage the development of strong basal growths and to form an open-centred plant with an evenly spaced system of branches.

As we saw in the previous chapter, when a new hybrid tea rose is planted it is recommended that you should immediately cut all of its shoots back to around 6in (15cm) from the ground and always cut to an outward-facing bud. By early summer new shoots will have developed, and during late summer or early autumn the flowered stems should be tipped back and any soft, unripe shoots cut out.

The following winter start the routine annual pruning by cutting out dead and diseased wood, followed by the removal of any inward-growing or crossing stems. Then cut back each shoot to between 6 and 9in (15 and 23cm) from ground level, or more for the less vigorous stems.

FLORIBUNDAS

The cluster-flowered bush roses, or floribundas, carry their blooms in 'heads' or 'clusters', and several blooms open at a time in each cluster.

Carry out the pruning at the same time as for hybrid teas, by cutting back all growths to three or five buds from the base. In terms of length this will be around 9 to 10in (23 to 25cm) from the ground. Floribundas are more vigorous than the hybrid teas, so generally they should be pruned less severely. At the same time, remove any suckers, and cut out all weak, damaged, or moribund shoots.

At the end of the growing season, during mid-autumn, tip back the main flowering stems, and completely remove any soft, sappy shoots.

ABOVE **A floribunda rose at maturity, showing the points where it should be pruned.**

ABOVE **The same rose after pruning. Note that the roots should be pruned if the rose is being newly planted or transplanted.**

ABOVE **Hybrid tea roses are pruned back each year, with shoots being cut back to between 6–9in (15–23cm) from the ground.**

MINIATURE AND PATIO ROSES

Most miniatures are 15in (38cm) high, or under, and both flowers and leaves are small, yet in proportion with the rest of the plant. Their pruning is basically similar to that recommended for hybrid teas, although one should not cut back newly planted miniatures too drastically.

Occasionally strong, over-vigorous shoots are thrown up, which will spoil the overall look of the plant. It is better to remove these entirely when pruning, so that the plant has a proper balanced framework throughout the growing season. As usual, deadheading is an important task, but do not be too severe. Cut out weak shoots and tip back the stronger stems to about 10 to 15cm (4 to 6in) from the ground.

Patio roses are newer still, having been introduced to commerce as recently as the 1980s. They are essentially small floribundas, and are pruned in a similar way, though on a smaller scale.

Try to avoid damaging the leaves of all these smaller rose types, as it is unsightly, and a severe amount of damage can debilitate a plant.

ABOVE 'Apricot Sunblaze' is a miniature rose with a spicy fragrance – when newly planted, do not prune it too severely.

PRUNING CLIMBING AND RAMBLER ROSES

The difference between climbers and ramblers is that the former have larger flowers but smaller trusses and stiffer stems, while the latter have long pliable stems and bear trusses of smallish flowers. If you want to cover a wall or screen it is usually better to choose a climber, while ramblers can be used effectively to trail along the soil as ground cover, or can be trailed through old trees.

CLIMBING ROSES

Flowers are carried on the framework of mature wood, which should be maintained for as long as possible. The advice is the same for whatever type of structure the rose is climbing up.

At the start, set the trellis, series of wires, post or pillar in the ground before planting the rose to avoid unnecessary disturbance to the roots later. Also, undertake any root pruning at this stage, and prune any weak growth or damaged stems.

The first summer flowers will appear on laterals from the old wood, and new growth will have developed from the base of the plant. Deadhead all faded flower trusses.

In mid-winter (or slightly earlier if you prefer) cut back the flowered laterals and some new shoots to maintain the plant's symmetry. You should aim to retain five to seven of the best, well-placed growths. Remove as many as possible of the older stems that have already flowered. Regular pruning at this time should also consist of cutting out weak and damaged wood, and finally tying in the new shoots.

ABOVE 'Alchemist' is a climbing shrub rose with peach-apricot-coloured flowers. It should be pruned in early to mid-winter.

ABOVE In winter there are no leaves to get in the way and you can clearly see stems that need tying in.

RAMBLERS

These are, perhaps, more colourful than climbers at certain times, but there is only one flush of bloom. Growth is extremely vigorous and the flowers are carried on new wood, so each year the old wood should be completely removed.

At planting time, preferably during autumn or late winter, a rambler should have had a few of its weakest shoots removed completely, and the rest of the growths cut back to 9 to 15in (23 to 38cm). In spring, new shoots will start to develop and, as soon as they are of a suitable size, they should be trained into place on horizontal support wires. A few flowers will appear in the first year on lateral shoots.

With first-year and established plants, the annual pruning regime should begin immediately after flowering and the flowered shoots should be cut out so that the new basal shoots can be tied in place.

Before you make any cuts, untie all the stems from the supports so that you can see what you are doing. With an established rambler cut out the old wood completely, leaving about six new canes. If this would leave the plant virtually stripped of stems and foliage, save some of the old wood, but prune the side growths on them quite severely.

Cut each side shoot back to three buds – this would normally be some 1in (2.5cm) from the main cane. The harder you prune, the greater the chance of young stems growing from close to the base. Tie the stems that are retained back to the supports, spreading them evenly.

ABOVE **The larger, older and gnarled stems of a mature rambler will need to be cut out with the aid of sturdy loppers.**

ABOVE **After flowering, cut each side shoot of rambler roses to some 1in (2.5cm) from the main cane.**

PRUNING SHRUB ROSES

This is a surprisingly large group of plants. They are divided into species roses, modern shrub roses and old-fashioned (or old garden) roses. The latter group are further divided into groups with names like the damasks, moss roses, bourbons and gallicas; they are all extremely rewarding during early summer and again in autumn if they produce bright hips. They are particularly at home in informal gardens and where their graceful, perhaps arching stems may have a little more room to grow.

It is often recommended that a shrub or species rose should be left unpruned, to grow naturally and unrestricted. This will usually last well for a few years, but the plant will not, in the long run, supply the gardener with the optimum display of blooms.

The rose genus is vast, and includes many species with varying habits of growth and flowering. Most grow naturally by a system of replacement of the older flowering branches by young ones. The type of pruning depends largely on the vigour of the rose, and the extent of its ability to replace old wood.

Develop a framework of sturdy shoots: cutting a small number of the oldest branches each year, to leave strong new shoots to take their place, effectively renews this framework. At the same time you should aim to achieve an open-centred plant and, once a year, tip back all vigorous shoots and laterals.

PRUNING GROUND-COVER ROSES

Ground-cover roses, whether creeping ramblers or the slightly more upright modern shrub types, need very little pruning. Cut out any dead or diseased stems and tip-prune the main stems. Shorten any laterals if they extend over their intended boundary.

With the rambler types, the stems will often root where they touch the ground, in the style of brambles, the closely related pernicious 'weed'. This can be a convenient way to cover a bank, for example. But ensure you keep the plant under control, otherwise you will have a jungle of growth to get rid of.

ABOVE This shrub rose, 'Financial Times Centenary', was launched in 1988 by David Austin Roses, England.

ABOVE 'Suffolk' is a modern shrub ground-cover rose, with bright scarlet, single flowers. It needs little pruning.

PRUNING STANDARD ROSES

Long-stemmed, large-headed standard roses are both stylish and elegant. If properly trained and maintained, a standard rose can have a life span the same as any normal bush rose. So what is a standard exactly?

Hybrid tea or floribunda rose cultivars can be budded at the top of rose stems growing from a natural rootstock (usually *Rosa rugosa* or *R. laxa*) some 4ft (1.2m) in height, instead of at ground level. This bare length of stem provides extra height, which is so desirable in flower beds and borders where an extra dimension and focal point are required.

Whereas a bush rose may be pruned back to four or five buds from the base, a standard is pruned much less severely, perhaps to seven or eight buds from the graft union. In most other respects standards are pruned just like hybrid teas, even down to the removal of suckers.

The main stem should have no side growths, or feathers, so any shoots should be rubbed off as soon as they are seen.

Weeping standards are usually taller than normal rose standards, even having as much as 6ft (2m) of bare stem. Rambler rose scions are grafted onto the stems, but the long, flexible growth habit results in an attractive weeping feature. Wire training frames can be used to keep the head of the plant under control: tying in stray shoots is better than cutting them out and losing the flowering potential. It is important to keep the centre fairly open, as before, and always prune to an outward-facing bud. In late summer, prune by removing all the shoots that have flowered during the past season. This will leave the younger growth, which will carry next year's flowers.

RIGHT **Standard roses, in general, are pruned in the same way as hybrid tea and floribunda roses – except that the head of stems is some 4ft (1.2m) above the ground.**

DEADHEADING ROSES

All cultivated flowering plants should be 'dead-headed', which means that the faded flowers should be removed before the plant has created the seed which follows. By doing this you are saving a huge amount of energy from being wasted, and it can either encourage more flowers in the same year, or help to build up the plant for better flowering the following year.

With some roses, deadheading can be combined with reducing the height of flowering stems during late summer or early autumn: use a pair of secateurs to cut off about a third of the flowering – this can equate to approximately 6 to 12in (15 to 30cm) of the fading flower head. Reducing the height of shoots by this much is often recommended for hybrid teas and floribundas, to prevent the plant being rocked about by the high autumn winds.

Faded flowers on first-year roses and most shrub roses should be removed with very little stem. Do not deadhead those varieties grown for their decorative hips.

ROSE SUCKERS

Suckers occur naturally on a host of garden trees and shrubs, and frequently from the rootstocks of grafted plants (it is perhaps in the rose border that this most commonly applies). When growing out from a plant's roots, suckers should be traced back to the original point of growth and then cut off. The surrounding tissue should also be pared away, to remove dormant buds nearby.

Suckers should always be removed, as they are both unsightly and an unnecessary drain on the plants' energies. Good nurserymen clean off suckers before displaying or sending out their plants, but mistakes can – and do – occur and I have seen some roses for sale with horrendously large suckers very evident. Therefore, inspect the subject before you plant it, and remove cleanly any knob-like shoot on the roots.

Fortunately it is relatively easy to identify rose suckers amongst a mass of foliage, as their leaves are usually light green, rounder than the true leaves, and quite distinct, especially when among roses with dark green or bronzy leaves.

ABOVE **Deadhead roses by cutting off the faded bloom, and a portion of stem down to the first node.**

ABOVE **Many gardeners prefer to pull suckers away from the rootstock, by gripping and yanking by hand.**

With standard and half-standard roses on a wide-spreading rootstock, such as *Rosa rugosa*, suckers may appear some distance away from the plants, and this can lead to confusion. However, they generally originate just under the soil surface, and can be traced back for removal. When suckers occur on stems of standard roses, they are best rubbed off, if noticed, while still young.

In the main, roses are grafted or budded, but occasionally they will be raised on their own roots (more often the case with climbers, shrub or species roses raised from cuttings or seed). In all of these, shoots coming from beneath the ground can be allowed to grow, for they will not be suckers.

Remove suckers with a knife as soon as you spot them, which will probably first be around late spring.

Sever the suckers at the point where they join the rootstock – it may be necessary to scrape some soil away to see where this is. Many gardeners prefer to pull the suckers off the rootstock, by gripping hard and yanking them so they come away at the base. Indeed, this is the way I was taught to do it by experts. It is an effective method, but requires a certain amount of strength and stamina if there are lots to do, and there are two minor risks: the first is that you may break the sucker so that there is not much left to pull, meaning that you end up cutting it anyway, and the second is that the plant may be dislodged in its planting position.

There are little hand tools available for de-suckering roses, but these are only really of use to those with a great many rose bushes to tackle.

ABOVE **When a bed of roses has been neatly pruned, cleared, weeded, tidied and mulched with a good-quality compost or manure, there is a great sense of satisfaction, and promise of flowers to come.**

CHAPTER 5

Weeds, pests and diseases

In the years immediately following the Second World War, the rose became globally popular, particularly in the UK and US. People wanted colour and fragrance in their lives, and they saw that roses provided both of these. In the 1950s and 60s, the rose became a symbol of a bright new future.

Thirty years later, however, when other types of all-singing-and-all-dancing flowering plants had been bred and promoted by the marketing experts, the rose declined in popularity. Apart from competition from other types of plant, it was widely reported that a reason for this decline was the fact that roses were 'high-maintenance': they always seemed to be getting diseases; they always needed to be sprayed against pests; and weeding through them was difficult because of their nasty thorns. Roses, it was frequently said, were more trouble than they were worth.

The truth, of course, is that all plants are susceptible to pests and diseases, and roses are no exception. There are, to help us out, an increasing number of new varieties that are being bred for resistance to certain diseases, and unlike 50 years ago there are some very effective controls available today. But by far and away the best way to prevent pests and diseases is to practice good husbandry – a lovely old gardening term, meaning to cultivate sensibly and 'hygienically'. In gardening, the word 'hygiene' is used in the context of keeping an area clean of unwanted plants, weeds, moss, algae and debris, all of which could be the breeding grounds for pests and diseases.

ABOVE **The clear yellow hybrid tea 'Freedom' AGM is largely regarded as one of the healthiest of roses.**

WEED CONTROL

The starting point has to be to keep your rose garden, rose beds and any other areas of your garden as free from weeds as possible. Unfortunately there is no simple, magical cure for the problem of weeds, but the important thing to realize is that by allowing them to grow, you will, unwittingly, be allowing and encouraging a number of pests and diseases to get a hold. Many types of weed are host plants for the breeding of aphids, and others make the ideal homes for diseases like rust and mildew.

Some weeds are annuals, and these can generally be kept in check by hoeing, mulching and spraying. The more troublesome weeds, however, are the perennial weeds, examples of which are ground elder, couch grass (or twitch), bindweed, docks, thistles and perennial nettles. These will all come up year after year if left to their own devices.

When you are first planting your roses, make sure that the ground is completely weed-free – particularly important if perennial weeds are present. If you have an area covered with couch grass, for example, the best course of action is to spray the area with a herbicide based on glyphosate, which will kill all parts of the plant it is sprayed on to. Happily, it becomes inactive on contact with the soil, and it is not taken up by the roots of any plant, no matter how close to the area of spray.

WEED SEED CONTROL

To prevent new weed seedlings appearing amongst roses, use only those products, probably based on simazine, that carry the manufacturer's recommendations for use with roses. Apply in spring, when the soil is firm and moist – the chemical acts as a sort of sealant over the soil, preventing weed seeds from germinating, and it should remain active for the whole growing season. Before applying, remove any weeds by hand. Or, if they are very

ABOVE **Weed growth makes any garden look unappealing and unkempt, and when weeds grow amongst roses, they are more difficult to control.**

small, hoe lightly or apply a contact weedkiller such as paraquat, but do not allow this chemical to come into contact with the roses. Then prune the roses and apply a fertilizer. Only then should you apply the simazine-based control. Finish off by applying a mulch (see next page).

PERENNIAL WEED CONTROL

It is always best to remove perennial weeds by hand, digging out as much of the root as possible. However, if they cover large areas, or you do not fancy braving the rose thorns to get in and tackle the weeds at close quarters, you could spray with a weedkiller based on dichlobenil. Apply when the soil is moist, and in spring, before the leaves start to unfurl.

At the rates at which it can safely be used near roses, some perennial weeds (such as ground elder and couch grass) will be checked or progressively controlled. Other, deeper-rooting weeds may not be checked sufficiently to see them off, so hand-weeding – but wearing gloves – is best for these.

Dichlobenil will also control germinating weed seedlings – and established annual weeds – for up to six months after application.

If couch and other grass weeds are your main problem, apply a weedkiller based on alloxydim-sodium. It is foliage-acting, non-residual and harmless to non-grassy plants, so it will not matter if you inadvertently get some on your roses.

MULCHING

Applying a spring mulch, following a fertilizer application, is essential to good rose growing, since it assists weed control by encouraging strong, healthy growth and dense leaf cover, which help to suppress weeds growing from wind- or bird-carried seeds. In theory, applying a good, thick mulch, topped up each spring, should keep a rose bed almost entirely free of weeds. This means you could practically dispense with the use of chemical weedkillers after a year or two.

ABOVE Thistles are perennial weeds which, once established, are difficult to control.

ABOVE Mulching around roses will condition the soil, conserve moisture and help to prevent weed growth.

The best mulches are organic, and made from well-rotted farm manure, leaf-mould, garden compost or processed bark. Soil bacteria and earthworms will make use of these materials, and the structure of the soil will be improved by their continued use.

Persistent perennial weeds may grow through these mulches, but they will root into the mulch, and because it has a much more open structure they are easier to remove.

Black polythene sheeting can be used as a surface mulch, but this is unsightly and is usually only seen in commercial nurseries, where the aesthetics of the rose beds are not as important as growing clean and healthy plants for sale to amateur gardeners.

RIGHT Mulching between roses with black plastic or other horticultural fabric is more commonly seen in commercial nurseries.

BELOW Cocoa mulch, derived from cocoa bean shells removed during the making of chocolate, is a modern material for conditioning the soil.

PESTS

There are various types of insect that prey on roses, and they are more prevalent in some countries than others. The three most common types, which are found universally on roses, are aphids, thrips and leaf-rolling sawfly.

APHIDS

These are the greenfly or blackfly that we see around the garden, infesting a whole range of garden plants. The aphids that attack your sweet peas, broad beans, or butterfly bushes may be a slightly different species of aphid, but the insects are not always fussy as to the type of plant they feed off, so all should be controlled as soon as they are seen.

Aphids feed by sucking the sap of tender plant growths. They are often seen clustering on young, unopened rose buds, and also on the undersides of young leaves. Their feeding will not kill an established rose bush, but it will distort the buds and leaves, and this can certainly ruin the appearance and flowering potential of a rose for the whole season.

Aphids also excrete honeydew, which attracts a black fungus called sooty mould which looks unsightly and, in severe cases, will debilitate a rose but not actually kill it.

Small infestations of aphids should be cut away, and the infested parts thrown in the bin. Larger infestations should be sprayed. There are many insecticides and modern systemic aphicides available today, and they all vary slightly in their formulations and their prices. A typical garden centre or shop will have a selection, and you should read the labels to decide on the best product for your situation.

ABOVE LEFT Greenfly feed by sucking the sap of tender young leaves, stems and buds.

LEFT Blackfly, in small infestations, should be cut out and thrown away; larger infestations should be sprayed.

THRIPS

These are small, narrow-bodied, sap-sucking insects. They feed on rose flowers, both as the grubs (larvae) and as winged adults. They are found in most countries, but are particularly troublesome in the US and Australia.

The larvae dig deep into the buds and eat the petal tissues inside. If, when a rosebud opens, you notice that the expanding petals are deformed and damaged, the plant will most certainly be suffering with thrips.

The adults, on the other hand, are carried on the wind and seem more attracted to pale-coloured rose varieties, such as whites, creams and pale pinks.

Control is not easy. Natural predators, such as birds, are seldom enough to control thrips, as the little pests spend much of their time buried deep inside a rose flower or bud – out of sight and where chemicals can't easily get to them. Insecticides are available however, and some control is provided when treating for other insects, such as aphids.

LEAF-ROLLING SAWFLY

This has become quite a common pest in some parts, particularly in gardens where there are sheltered corners, and trees where the flies seem to like to hover.

Tightly rolled individual leaves are a sign of their presence. Badly infected leaves will shrivel and die and, inside the roll, you will find the green-grey maggot of the sawfly. Picking off the rolled leaves by hand, and squeezing the leaves tightly to dispatch the grub inside, can control small-scale infestations. Chemical sprays are available, and are best applied in mid- to late spring.

ABOVE **Tightly rolled leaves are a sure sign of the presence of the rose leaf-rolling sawfly.**

LEAFHOPPERS, RED SPIDER MITES CATERPILLARS AND LEAF-CUTTER BEES

There are a few other pests that commonly attack roses, but they are of less significance than those mentioned previously.

The leafhopper is a small, yellowish insect, which causes patches of rose leaves to become pale and mottled. You may find their empty white skins on the undersides of leaves. In severe cases they will check the growth of a rose, and cause early defoliation.

Red spider mites are minute and distinctly yellowish. They cause bronze patches on the upper surfaces of leaves, and you may find very fine webbing between the leaves and stems. Attacks are worst when the weather is hot and dry. Leafhoppers and spider mites can be controlled chemically.

There are a number of different caterpillar species that will readily devour rose foliage. One of the worst is the caterpillar of the winter moth, seen as bright green caterpillars some ½in (1cm) long. If they are not too numerous, pick them off by hand. Otherwise, spray with a suitable insecticide.

Finally, the leaf-cutter bee cuts regular-shaped holes at the sides of rose leaves, then carries the pieces back to its nest. It does not harm the plant, other than disfiguring a small number of leaves. It is not worth controlling it chemically: you could destroy the nests if you come across them, but this will merely send the bee off elsewhere.

ABOVE The leaf-cutter bee cuts round-shaped holes at the edges of rose leaves, then flies off to its nest with the leaf piece.

ABOVE There are a number of different caterpillar species that will readily devour rose leaves.

ABOVE Red spider mites cause bronze patches on the upper surfaces of rose leaves. They are worst in hot, dry conditions.

ABOVE The leafhopper causes patches on rose leaves to become pale and mottled. In severe cases they can cause leaves to drop.

DISEASES

The three main diseases to affect roses are blackspot, rust and mildew. These fungal infections are unsightly, but are not fatal to a well-established plant. The severity of their infection will vary from year to year, and this could be due either to cultivation or climate. For example, a rose may be mildewed badly one year because it had been weakened by bad cultivation, but another year, when its needs have been properly met, it may be perfectly free from the disease. Similarly, blackspot may be more severe in a damp, cool year, and practically non-existent in a hot, dry summer.

BLACKSPOT

This fungal disease shows up, quite literally, as black spots on the rose leaves. The leaves will then turn yellow prematurely, and drop off. A severe infestation will cause a plant to defoliate completely, possibly several months before the leaves would naturally die and drop. The disease also affects other parts of the plant, and overwinters on the stems, which makes it difficult to prevent new infection the following year. The fungal spores are carried on the wind, and these will settle and grow on healthy plants, particularly in cooler, wetter weather. Plants are weakened by blackspot, and young plants may even be killed outright.

Healthy plants are always less vulnerable to blackspot, so keep plants well nourished and watered. In the case of rose blackspot, prevention is certainly better than cure, and the best way to prevent it is to buy varieties that show a degree of resistance to it, such as the 'Flower Carpet' series. Also, to make sure that all fallen rose leaves at the end of the season are gathered up and disposed of, preferably by burning, to avoid any overwintering spores from re-infecting in the new season.

It is also better to avoid certain varieties, such as 'Lilli Marlene' and 'American Beauty', which are more susceptible to blackspot. The Directory section of this book (see pages 86–155) specifies whether the varieties included are particularly vulnerable, or resistant, to certain diseases.

ABOVE **Typically, blackspot shows on the leaves, but the fungal spores can survive on stems, and overwinter on foliage on the ground. Fortunately, many new roses are bred to be resistant to it.**

MILDEW

There are two different types of mildew. The first – and more pertinent form where garden roses are concerned – is powdery mildew, which is identified by the way it covers young leaves, buds and stems with its white 'mycelium' (older parts of the plant are generally resistant to mildew). Without treatment, the disease will cause the affected parts to become stunted and distorted.

ABOVE **Mildew spores are carried on the wind, and readily infest plants that are slightly dehydrated.**

The spores are carried on the wind, and they will most readily infest plants that are slightly dehydrated, or if there is poor air circulation in the vicinity of the plant, for example where climbing roses are growing against walls (these types of rose, in general, are more susceptible, for this reason). Cool, wet weather makes the ideal conditions for the spores to germinate.

Fortunately, the disease is rarely fatal to roses. Fungicidal sprays are available but, as stated earlier, plants with the best health are most likely to avoid infection. It is important to water the plants regularly, especially in times of drought.

Avoid the most susceptible types of rose, such as 'Madame Isaac Pereire' AGM and 'Empereur du Maroc'.

The second type of mildew is known as downy mildew, which is characterized by greyish brown pustules on the undersides of the leaves. It is less of a problem with roses growing outdoors, but can be a serious problem for growers of roses under glass or in polytunnels (for example commercial growers who grow roses for the cut-flower trade).

RUST

This fungal disease is very aptly named, for the tell-tale signs are bright orange, rust-like pustules that start to appear on both sides of the leaves, and which then spread to other parts of the plant. Like most fungal diseases of plants, rust spreads most rapidly in damp, cool weather.

The disease is hard to eradicate because it overwinters as spores on the soil, as well as on fallen leaves – and not just rose leaves. Wind-blown spores also bring in new infection. Chemical sprays are available, and it is best to apply them early in the season, before any signs of the rust become apparent.

Avoid the most susceptible types of rose, such as the older rugosa varieties like 'Conrad Ferdinand Meyer' and the floribunda variety 'Fashion'.

ROSE BALLING

This is not as common as the other diseases mentioned, but is still caused by fungal infection, and is most severe in a cool, wet season. It affects the flowers, and only the flowers, just as they are about to open from buds.

It manifests itself as an invisible covering of fungal mycelium, effectively sticking the surface of the petals together.

Sometimes it is possible to 'massage' the bud manually. This can un-stick the petals, and the resulting flower may be only slightly damaged, with the outer petals coming off worst.

Rose balling is a problem mostly with roses that are many petalled, and thinner petalled. This usually means that roses popular more than a hundred years ago are most susceptible, as modern-day varieties generally have been bred to possess thicker, sturdier petals. The old gallica rose 'Empress Josephine', the bourbon rose 'Souvenir de la Malmaison', and hybrids of *Rosa rugosa* and *R. spinosissima* are the most susceptible.

USING SPRAYS

Finally, a word about the use of sprays, which applies to the whole garden, not just the rose bed: when applying pesticides and herbicides, it is essential that they are distributed both accurately and uniformly. Not only does this ensure the safety of the plants, but it is also what I call the three 'E's: the most effective, the most economical and most environmentally appropriate approach. Follow these three simple guidelines to achieve this:

- only spray on a still day, for spray drift caused by the wind can cause havoc.
- if possible, spray in early morning or in the evening, as this is when flying insects are most inactive; bees and other beneficial creatures can sometimes be harmed by these chemicals, and we should avoid indiscriminate harm to them.
- always follow the manufacturer's instructions when it comes to mixing, dosage and application – large amounts of concentrated chemicals can harm plants, soil and animal life, and therefore be unpleasant for all of us.

ABOVE **Balling of rose flowers is most common during a cool, wet season, and on varieties with many thin petals.**

ABOVE **Spray roses early in the morning or in the evening, as this is when beneficial insects, such as bees, are most inactive.**

CHAPTER 6

Propagating roses

To hobby gardeners, raising plants – and particularly increasing stocks of plants – is an integral part of the hobby. There are few aspects of gardening more satisfying than the sight of a haze of green seedlings appearing in pots and trays, or new roots forming on bits of stems. However, in the case of roses, the need to raise and propagate new plants does not generally apply; amateur gardeners propagate fewer roses than almost any other major plant group – instead, they tend to keep a rose until it dies, and then they buy a replacement variety.

Named rose bush varieties are almost always budded or grafted onto the rootstocks from different roses, which gives the named plants their vigour and habit. This is not something that the amateur gardener needs to worry about. And, apart from the species, there are very few types of rose that will come true from seed, so it is not really worth going to the trouble of saving the seed and growing it. Neither is it very common to see rose seeds for sale, from which you can grow your own plants. However, if you fancy trying your hand at rose propagation, these few pages will be of interest. Just don't expect too much!

LEFT Rose hips – themselves an important feature of some rose species and varieties – are the 'fruits' which contain seeds.

ROSES FROM SEED

Seed is the best way to raise large quantities of species roses for hedging, or as rootstocks. If you are hoping to breed a new variety – which requires hybridizing (or 'crossing' one type of rose with another, and sowing the seed of the offspring) – you should be prepared for many years of painstaking record-keeping, and throwing away of unwanted plants.

Many worthy rose varieties have originated from seedlings from lucky crosses, but the likelihood of finding anything worthwhile by chance is remote. Even rose breeders have to grow hundreds of seedlings, and to nurture them for three or more years (that is, to flowering size) then perform lengthy year-long tests for durability, disease-resistance, weather-tolerance, fragrance and so on. Finally, they will then end up with just a handful of roses that are worth discussing with a commercial grower with a view to mass production – a term called 'bulking out'.

It is not unusual for it to take ten years of development to get a new rose variety to market. Growing roses from seed is not, therefore, something the average gardener should contemplate unless aware of the drawbacks, although the seed-sowing process itself is not difficult.

Rose hips should be collected in early winter, when they are fully ripe, and the seeds – which in most cases are hard, white pips – should be carefully separated and washed away from the flesh. Store the dry seeds in an airtight container, in a refrigerator as, like most hardy trees and shrubs, rose seeds need a period of chilling before they will germinate. In fact, seed of the alpine rose species *Rosa glauca* needs two years or more outdoors, exposed to all weathers, before it will germinate.

In early spring sow your rose seed shallowly in a gritty, soil-based compost. If you use a seed tray divided into modules, you should sow one seed per compartment. Cover the compost lightly with gravel, or perlite, to prevent the seeds from being washed away by the rain. Leave the containers in a cool greenhouse or coldframe, or even outside in sheltered areas.

Germination should occur sporadically after a month or six weeks. When the seedlings are large enough to be handled, pot them up into individual pots.

ABOVE **Collect the hip in early winter, when it is fully ripe; remove the seeds and wash them so that they are properly separated from the flesh.**

HARDWOOD CUTTINGS

This is the easiest way to propagate roses, but modern varieties – especially floribundas and hybrid teas – strike less readily than species roses and older varieties.

METHOD

◆ Being careful to avoid the thorns, cut lengths of the current year's healthy shoots some 6 to 8in (15 to 20cm) long in mid- to late autumn, and trim them to just above a bud at the top and just below one at the bottom. There should be at least three or four nodes along the length of each cutting.

◆ Insert these cuttings vertically into the soil, to approximately half their length, preferably in a sheltered part of the garden, or a coldframe. Firm them slightly, so they will not be blown over by the wind.

◆ They should form roots within six to nine months, but it is best not to transplant or pot up the young plants until the following autumn.

ABOVE **The hardwood cutting should be some 6–8in (15–20cm) long, and trimmed just above a bud at the top and just below one at the bottom.**

ABOVE **The trimmed cutting should have at least three or four nodes along its length.**

ABOVE **When taking cuttings, it is important to select only healthy wood; check it thoroughly before cutting it from the plant.**

ABOVE **A single rose should offer three or four decent-sized cuttings; these are now ready for inserting, vertically, into the soil.**

SOFTWOOD CUTTINGS

These can be taken at any time from late spring until mid-autumn. Perhaps the best timing, however, is soon after the plants have had their first flowering. The stems are not entirely fleshy at this time, but yet not too woody either.

METHOD

◆ With a sharp knife, trim the cuttings so that they are about 4in (10cm) long, and with a number of closely spaced buds near the base. These will break to form new shoots below the surface of the compost. Always keep at least one leaf – and preferably two or three leaves – at the top.

◆ Dip the base of each cutting in a hormone rooting powder containing a fungicide, to stop the stem from rotting. Use a free-draining potting compost and water the cuttings in.

◆ Cover the pot with a plastic bag and put in a warm, semi-shaded place, such as a windowsill that receives little direct sunlight.

ABOVE **When taking softwood cuttings, select the young pliable shoot tips that have not yet become too woody.**

LAYERING

Any rose with sufficiently flexible stems can be layered in the autumn. Choose a low-growing shoot, and make a slight horizontal cut with a sharp, clean knife. Peg the shoot down into the soil, ideally with a rock or other weight placed on top. Water the area and forget about it for around a year. By then, the shoot should have produced roots, and you can sever it from the parent plant.

MICROPROPAGATION

Many of today's popular roses, mass-produced for commerce, are propagated in this way. Although it is not really practical to do this at home, it is an interesting technique to follow.

In simple terms, tiny fragments of living tissue are removed from a plant under carefully controlled, clinically sterile conditions, and these pieces are placed on to a nutrient jelly and incubated. The tissue develops into a miniature plant, which is then transferred to more conventional potting compost. The plant is hardened off and eventually offered for sale.

'Microprop', as it is known, usually guarantees complete uniformity among the progeny And, provided that the original 'mother' plant was free from virus, it also offers the grower the ability to produce plants free from virus contamination. This is important for individual plants, of course, but in commercial terms it enables plants to be guaranteed healthy and they are then allowed to be exported to countries where health regulations are more rigorous.

CHAPTER 7

Year-round care

Despite the second half of this book being highly pictorial, describing more than a hundred of our most popular rose species and cultivars, and despite the first half of this book giving in-depth detail on the designing, planting, pruning and propagation of roses, it would not surprise me at all if this particular chapter is the most thumbed-through of the entire book.

This will certainly be the case if you are new to rose growing, for over the next eight pages you will discover precisely when you need to be doing things to – and in – your rose beds.

The gardening year is divided into 12; by all means think of them as 'months', but I am not going to label them 'January', 'February' and so on. This is because – depending on where you live – the weather for, say, October may be considerably warmer for you than another reader at the opposite end of the country. So it is far more accurate to refer to the 12 divisions seasonally.

If you put into practice the information contained here, your rose plants and, dare I say, rose 'gardens' will give an optimum performance every year.

ABOVE **A beautiful rose garden is not difficult to achieve, as long as you follow a year-round maintenance programme.**

ABOVE Roses may be planted in early winter, if soil conditions are favourable.

ABOVE True climbing roses (not ramblers) may be pruned in mid-winter, as shown here.

EARLY WINTER

Prepare the soil: new rose beds may be dug, and old ones renovated, in time for any new rose plants you intend to acquire. The soil needs time to settle, so do not plant anything yet (for more details on this, see pages 40–2).

Plant: having said that, new roses may be planted on a day when the soil is not frozen or waterlogged, on ground that was prepared a month or two previously. But before you dig the holes and plant them, give the area a final application of bonemeal fertilizer at 2oz per yd^2 (65g per m^2), working this into the surface, treading the ground firm, and then raking it level (see pages 43–7).

Underplant: if you are planning to grow low plants amongst your roses, it is a good idea to plant those at the same time. However, it isn't always convenient – or they may not be available if, for example, you plan to use summer bedding plants – in which case, aim to plant them as soon as possible.

MID-WINTER

Plant: roses may be planted on soil that was prepared a month or two previously – it should be dressed (as detailed above), just prior to planting (see pages 43–7).

Prune climbing roses: true climbing roses may be pruned at this time, but leave ramblers until late summer. Thriving plants will have produced a number of strong shoots during the previous summer, and the aim should be to keep five to seven strong, well-placed growths. Remove as many as possible of the older stems that have flowered (see page 56).

Prune shrub roses: weather permitting, these roses may be pruned now. Although heavy pruning is not required, some restriction in size can be beneficial, particularly if you have a small garden (see page 58).

ABOVE **Rabbits are very active in late winter and it is at this time that they can do most damage to garden plants.**

LATE WINTER

Prune bush roses: it does not matter if you live in a warm or cold area, this is the best time to prune hybrid teas, floribundas, miniatures, patio and ground-cover roses (if they need it); the only stipulation is that you should avoid doing it in frosty weather (see Chapter 4, pages 48–61).

Control weeds and pests: after pruning, weed the rose beds (see pages 63–5) and spray the plants with a fungicide as a precaution against mildew and blackspot (see pages 69–70). Make sure that every stem and shoot is well covered with the spray.

Control rabbits: these can cause significant damage to roses, mainly to the fresh growths that emerge after pruning – particularly if you live in a rural area. You may wish to erect a barrier of wire netting, some 3ft (90cm) high, around your plants and/or rose bed at this time; turn the bottom 6in (15cm) of the wire mesh outwards, and bury it under the soil or turf. This will help to safeguard your plants. It is advisable to leave the barrier in place for at least two months, or until the worst of the rabbit activity has passed.

EARLY SPRING

Feed: roses planted in well-manured soil do not require a dressing of fertilizer in spring. Established roses, however, should be given a feed, using a balanced fertilizer. Always check the application rates on the side of the packet. Rake or hoe the feed into the top inch or two (3 to 5cm) of the soil.

Mulch: once the roses have started to grow, and the soil has become warmer, a mulch of organic material will help to nourish the plants, conserve moisture in the soil and suppress weed growth. Cow or horse manure, spent mushroom or normal garden compost may be used, but in every case it must be well-rotted. A layer 2 to 3in (5 to 8cm) deep is needed for effective results, but do not allow the material to lay against the stems of the roses, as it may 'burn' the plant tissue. Wait until the soil is moist after a rain before applying it. Although both old and new roses will benefit from a mulch, if you have a short supply you should apply it to the most needy, which are likely to be the older plants.

Weed: the mulching described above will go a long way to controlling weeds in your rose bed. Failing that, however, you will need to weed by hand, or with the use of chemicals. In either case, a concerted effort now will pay dividends later; effective weed control in early spring will result in fewer weeds setting seed (see pages 63–5).

Control aphids: shrub roses are particularly susceptible to attacks by greenfly and blackfly, even at this early stage in the growing year. Spray with a suitable insecticide as soon as any appear (see page 66).

Sow seed of roses: see page 73.

ABOVE Established roses should be given a feed in early spring, and again in early summer.

ABOVE Mid-spring is a key period for controlling insect pests, such as aphids.

MID-SPRING

Plant: there is still time to replace any roses that were damaged or killed during the winter. For this time of year you should plant only container-grown varieties, as they can be placed in the planting holes without disturbing the roots. See pages 46–7 for detailed planting instructions.

Control pests and diseases: continue to look for – and control – aphids. These insects breed at an alarming rate, unless they are spotted at an early stage and action is taken immediately. This is a key period for controlling insect pests such as caterpillars and leaf-rolling sawfly, and rose diseases such as blackspot (see pages 66–71).

Weed: continue to remove weeds or apply herbicides as necessary.

ABOVE **Tie in stems of climbing roses as they develop; leave them too long and they will not be flexible enough.**

ABOVE **Take the opportunity to enjoy the fragrance of roses which, depending on variety, may be soon after the buds open.**

LATE SPRING

Tie in climbing roses: as new stems on these plants develop, they should be tied to their supports to prevent wind damage. If this is done regularly, they should be in position to replace the older wood, which will be pruned out during the following mid-winter. Left untied they may well break, or be difficult to tie later on because they have become inflexible.

Remove suckers: suckers come from below the graft union, which is visible as a swelling near the base of the rose stem; they do not appear on roses grown on their own roots, such as species roses. These frequently have greater vigour than the main plants and, if left, will take over. They will not have the same traits as the main plant, and they rarely flower. Suckers must be removed whenever they are seen, but they will become most evident during this period (see pages 60–1).

Pests and diseases: continue to keep a lookout for signs of infestation or infection: never let these gain a firm hold. Spray as necessary.

Take softwood cuttings: see page 75.

EARLY SUMMER

Sniff the roses: enjoy the peak of the rose-flowering year!

Feed: unless your soil is particularly fertile, established roses will benefit from another application of fertilizer. A balanced, general feed at the rate of 2oz per yd^2 (65g per m^2) will encourage further blooms. Do not apply this feed beyond early summer, as it will promote growth of young stems that will not ripen before the onset of colder weather.

Deadhead: the first flush of flowers will be over by now, and the sooner the dead blooms are removed the better. Cut down the flower stem by about one third (see page 60). Do not dead-head roses grown for their autumn hips.

Pests and diseases: rose sawfly may be troublesome around now. The larvae eat the inner tissue of leaves, reducing them to mere skeletons. Spray accordingly. Also, spray the top and undersides of leaves with a fungicide as a precaution against mildew. Once the white mildew appears, spraying is ineffective (see page 67).

ABOVE **Do not allow weeds to become large, or too numerous, as weeding between roses can be a painful process.**

Weed: continue to remove weeds (applying herbicides as necessary). Some weeds may have penetrated the mulch layer applied in early spring, but these should be relatively easy to remove. Soft thistles, which act as host plants for aphids, should be removed first.

Make notes: as you travel about you will see many roses in flower at this time. Whenever possible, note the names of varieties that you like so that you can read up about them, and perhaps order them later. Think about copying ideas, or making changes to the rose garden during the following winter. It is often better to visualize changes when the plants are at their most colourful.

Tie in climbing roses: continue to do this (see 'Late Spring').

Remove suckers: continue to do this (see 'Late Spring').

Take softwood cuttings: see page 75.

MID-SUMMER
Order new roses: around now all of the specialist rose nurseries are bringing out their mail-order catalogues for the forthcoming year. Choose your plants and place your orders early, particularly if you want newly launched varieties, as stocks may run out.

Deadhead: continue to do this (see 'Early Summer').

Pests and diseases: continue to control them (see 'Early Summer'). Aphids may be marginally less of a problem from now, but rose rust may be becoming evident (see page 70).

Tie in climbing roses: continue to do this (see 'Late Spring').

Take softwood cuttings: see page 75.

ABOVE **Continue to deadhead roses – by late summer the flowers do not seem to last long.**

ABOVE **It is worth spraying against pests and diseases throughout the early autumn.**

LATE SUMMER

Prune ramblers: late summer and into early autumn is the best time for pruning ramblers, but first untie all the stems from the supports, so that you can see what is what (see page 57).

Prune weeping standards: adopt the same basic pruning method as for ramblers. Remove any thin, damaged, diseased, or crossing branching, retaining as many healthy young growths as necessary.

Deadhead: continue to deadhead (see 'Early Summer'). Late summer flowers on modern rose varieties do not seem to last for long, and seedpods appear quickly at this time of year. Remove seedpods if they form before you get a chance to deadhead – unless they are varieties which are being grown especially because they colour up for autumn decoration.

Pests and diseases: continue to control these, including the fungal diseases blackspot and mildew (see 'Early Summer').

Tie-in climbing roses: continue to do this (see 'Late Spring').

Take softwood cuttings: see page 75.

EARLY AUTUMN

Make new rose beds: prepare the soil for new or replanted rose beds. If you are introducing roses to an area of your garden for the first time, then dig and dress the soil as discussed on page 41. If, however, you are replanting an area where roses have grown until this point, you should either change the top 12 to15in (30 to 38cm) of soil, or sterilize it chemically (see page 42).

Pests and diseases: when necessary, keep spraying against pests and diseases until mid-autumn, after which chemical controls become ineffective, as both the insect pests and the fungal problems will have gone past their active life cycles.

Take softwood cuttings: see page 75.

Layer roses: see page 75.

ABOVE Continue to remove dead leaves, and weeds such as the thistle, from established rose beds.

ABOVE From mid- to late autumn it is possible to take hardwood cuttings of favourite rose varieties.

MID-AUTUMN

Plant: as soon as plants arrive, unpack them and heel them in so that the roots do not dry out. Then, as soon as you are able, follow the planting procedures outlined on pages 44–5.

Prune: hybrid tea, floribunda, standard, miniature, patio and modern shrub roses may all be pruned now if you live in a mild, sheltered area (see Chapter 4, pages 48–61). Alternatively, some gardeners prefer to wait until late winter, when the hardest frosts are over.

Cut back: if you don't undertake a main pruning now, it is still worth cutting back any particularly long growths by half. This will reduce 'wind rock', a buffeting in the autumn and winter winds that can loosen the stem at ground level and allow water and frost to penetrate – sometimes with fatal results for the plant.

Hygiene: remove weeds and dead leaves from existing rose beds. Burn rose leaves if blackspot, mildew or rust have been present.

Take hardwood cuttings: see page 74.

Layer roses: see page 75.

LATE AUTUMN

Prepare the soil: new rose beds may be dug, and old ones renovated (see 'Early Winter').

Check supports: supports for standard roses, climbing roses and ramblers should always be firm, but the action of autumn frosts and winds – or simply old age – can cause them to be broken or otherwise unstable. Now is a good time to replace these where necessary. Also, check that ties are secure without being too tight.

Check equipment: if secateurs and pruners are not cutting cleanly, sharpen the angled side of the blade on a fine carborundum or oil stone. The same abrasive surface can be used for sharpening pruning or cutting knives. Afterwards, smear the blades with an oily rag, and put a drop of oil on pivots. If sprayers were put away uncleaned, rinse them with warm water containing a little detergent. Undo the spray nozzle and clean it thoroughly.

Hygiene: see 'Mid-autumn'.

Take hardwood cuttings: see page 74.

Layer roses: see page 75.

LEFT An old-style, traditional knot garden planting, with box edging and low-growing roses ('White Pet' AGM) as the infill.

CHAPTER 8

Directory of roses

This Directory is an invaluable source of reference, whether you are choosing roses to grow, or identifying roses you have seen and like. It includes descriptions of over one hundred of the most popular garden roses, and pictures of many of them, too. Under each of the descriptions are these items of information:

Origin This tells you, if known, how and where the variety of rose was bred, raised or discovered. In the case of rose breeding, there are a number of famous nurseries, breeders and specialists around the world.

For example, the Poulsen family from Denmark is Scandinavia's largest rose nursery, and produced its first series of classic roses a century ago.

The Kordes family from Germany is arguably the most distinguished rose family in Europe. The Kordes started their nursery in 1887 and have raised hundreds of roses, including the super-hardy Kordesii hybrids.

For six generations the the Meilland family from France have been breeding roses, and have been responsible for hundreds of popular cultivars, including probably the world's best-known rose, the royalties from which have made a fortune for the family. It was originally named 'Mme A. Meilland' (1942), but was marketed at the end of the Second World War under the name of 'Peace'. It caught the imagination of gardeners across the world as a symbol for a bright new beginning.

Other famous rose breeders include the Dickson, Harkness and Fryer nurseries, along with David Austin and Peter Beales (all UK), the McGredy family (Ireland and New Zealand), Werner Noack and Matthias Tantau (both Germany) and Weeks Roses (US).

Parentage To produce a 'thoroughbred' rose a breeder needs to select good offspring from high-quality plants. It is important, therefore, to know the cultivars or species that you are crossing, and how those crosses may also be used to create new plants. In many cases, the roses bear traits of one parent over another, or even of ancestors further back than one generation.

USDA zone These are the climate zones referred to on pages 24 and 25, designed to identify the relative hardiness of plants.

Description of bloom Here you will discover details of flower colour and shade, and whether the rose in question is single, semi-double, or double in structure.

Description of foliage Not all rose leaves are one of the many tones of green; a number of roses have red, bronze and coppery tints also.

Height and spread This will be useful when choosing and designing plants for a garden. All sizes are given for plants at maturity.

GROUND-COVER ROSES

These roses, also known as 'procumbent' roses, grow broader than than they do tall. They can fulfil a variety of roles in the garden, from underplanting in shrubberies, filling large beds and cascading down banks, to use in large pots and patio containers. A few ground-cover roses even produce long, lax, thorny stems, which can be used to climb up and through small trees and along fences, walls and trelliswork.

Most ground-cover roses form a dense, leafy mat, useful for hiding unsightly mounds and manhole covers. But apart for one or two exceptions, do not expect them to be good at eliminating weeds (unlike most other types of ground-cover plant), as rose growth is generally not sufficiently dense to prevent weeds taking hold. For this reason, it is important to dig out the roots of perennial weeds before you plant the roses.

NAME: 'AVON' AGM

Origin: Bred by Poulson, Denmark (1992)
Parentage: 'Pink Drift' x seedling
USDA zone: 5
Description of bloom: Semi-double, cupped, 1½in (4cm) across, in numerous clusters. Blush pink to white, with golden stamens. Repeats well
Scent: Light, vaguely 'musky'
Description of foliage: Mid-green, glossy
Height and spread: 4 x 6ft (1.2 x 2m)
This rose flowers almost continually from late spring to mid-autumn. The blooms come in clusters, typically of 5–10. Young plants are good for containers, but they will eventually get too big. It is therefore recommended that they are grown this way for their first year only, then planted out in their final positions in autumn.

NAME: 'BERKSHIRE' AGM

Origin: Bred by Kordes, Germany (1991)
Parentage: 'Partridge' x seedling
USDA zone: 5
Description of bloom: Semi-double, cupped 2in (5cm) across, freely borne in neat clusters. Cherry pink, with golden stamens in the centre
Scent: Light and fruity
Description of foliage: Dark bluish green, glossy and healthy
Height and spread: 2½ x 5ft (75 x 1.5m)

ABOVE 'Berkshire' AGM

One of the most eye-catching of all ground-cover roses, 'Berkshire' is known for the sheer abundance of its flowers. Each petal has a scalloped edge. Excellent for covering a sunny bank, but equally good growing in a container.

ABOVE '**Bonica' AGM**

ABOVE '**County of Yorkshire'**

NAME: 'BONICA' AGM

Origin: Meilland, France (1985)
Parentage: Probably (*Rosa sempervirens* x 'Mlle Marthe Carron') x 'Picasso'
USDA zone: 5
Description of bloom: Soft, rose pink. Double, cupped blooms 3in (8cm) across, carried in large clusters
Scent: Light and delicate
Description of foliage: Dark green; small, glossy and plentiful
Height and spread: 3¼ft x 4½ft (1 x 1.4m)
Flowering right through summer and autumn this is one of the finest and most floriferous of roses. Although classed as a double, it has a looser, almost semi-double flower, which starts opening from a soft, rose pink and fading almost to white as it ages. Although listed here under 'Ground-Cover', it is also sold as a shrub rose, for its habit is rather upright. Blooms are particularly good for cutting. It may be found for sale under the name 'Meidomonac' or 'Bonica 82'. In 1994, a sport of this rose was selected by the breeder, Meilland of France, and released under the name 'Royal Bonica'.

NAME: 'COUNTY OF HAMPSHIRE'

Origin: Bred by Kordes, Germany (2006)
Parentage: Not disclosed
USDA zone: 6
Description of bloom: Vibrant pink, button flowers 1½in (4cm) in diameter
Scent: Light
Description of foliage: Dark green; glossy
Height and spread: 2 x 3ft (60 x 90cm)
Flowers from late spring, through to the first frosts. It is recommended for mass planting, borders, containers and even windowboxes.

NAME: 'COUNTY OF YORKSHIRE'

Origin: Bred by Kordes, Germany (2006)
Parentage: Not disclosed
USDA zone: 6
Description of bloom: Dazzling white, semi-double blooms some 2in (5cm) in diameter
Scent: Light
Description of foliage: Deep green; glossy
Height and spread: 2 x 3ft (60 x 90cm)
Flowers are borne in great abundance on a ground-hugging bush with leaves that contrast well. Recommended for borders, containers and mass planting.

NAME: 'FERDY'

Origin: Suzuki, Japan (1984)
Parentage: Seedling x 'Petite Folie' seedling
USDA zone: 6
Description of bloom: Neat, semi-double flowers, coral pink at first, darkening to red, especially in hot weather
Scent: None
Description of foliage: Small, shiny, mid-green
Height and spread: 4¾ x 4¾ft (1.4 x1.4m)

Not such a common rose, in the main because it has no scent, but also because it has just one flowering period. However, when it is in full flower it is stunning, covering itself with blooms so that hardly a leaf is seen. Petals do not usually drop when the flowers fade, and the temptation is to go over the plant with a pair of shears to tidy it up. However, if you do this too severely, you will be forfeiting much of the flower for the following year. Little or no pruning suits this rose best.

NAME: 'FLOWER CARPET'

Origin: Noack, Germany (1989)
Parentage: 'Immensee' x 'Amanda'
USDA zone: 5
Description of bloom: Open-cupped, loosely double. For colours, see below
Scent: Light and musky
Description of foliage: Dark, glossy green
Height and spread: 2½ x 3¼ft (80cm x 1m)

The original 'Flower Carpet' was deep pink, almost crimson at first (the buds being red), with a small white eye. In subsequent years yellow, white and paler pink versions were launched into the market. When buying from a garden centre or mail order supplier you need to specify the colour you want. This is truly a magnificent rose, as it needs little in the way of pruning, grows well in poor soil (responding to just a little feed and water in hot weather) and, even better, seems resistant to blackspot, rust and mildew. It is often used in municipal planting schemes where the plants are left to fend for themselves,

ABOVE **'Flower Carpet' (pink)**

with very little in the way of maintenance. This suggests that it is ideal for the low-maintenance garden. Sometimes this rose is also found under the name 'Heidetraum'.

NAME: 'HERTFORDSHIRE' AGM

Origin: Kordes, Germany (1989)
Parentage: Not disclosed
USDA zone: 5
Description of bloom: Deep pink, single flowers, with a white patch in the centre and a circle of yellow stamens. The pink blooms turn to red as they age ►

ABOVE **'Hertfordshire' AGM**

Scent: Light and pleasant
Description of foliage: Plentiful, small and a glossy, rich green
Height and spread: 18in x 3¼ft (45cm x 1m)
This is a good repeat-flowerer, and the flowers come in large clusters, typically in groups of 20 to 30. Recommended for a border front, sunny bank, or for cascading over the sides of a large container. It has a long season of colour and needs little in the way of pruning. Sometimes sold under the name 'Tommelise'.

NAME: **'MAX GRAF'**

Origin: Natural hybrid discovered in Bowditch Nursery, Connecticut, US (1919)
Parentage: *Rosa wichurana* x *Rosa rugosa*
USDA zone: 5
Description of bloom: Dark pink, fading to rose pink, with a central boss of yellow stamens
Scent: Light and musky

Description of foliage: Dark, glossy green
Height and spread: 20in x 13ft (50cm x 4m)
Flowers come rather late in the season, but the volume of them makes a real impact. Branches trail outwards, creeping along the ground in the style of *R. wichurana*. They are also covered in fierce, brown prickles, which come more from the *R. rugosa* side of the parentage. Although sold and grown more often than not as a ground-cover rose, it does not have the ability to smother perennial weeds as many ground-cover roses do. Also, being prickly, it is not easy to get into in order to weed. It is completely immune to blackspot.

NAME: **'NIPPER'**

Origin: Harkness, UK (1997)
Parentage: Not disclosed
USDA zone: 6
Description of bloom: Medium red fully double ▶

ABOVE **'Nipper'**

Scent: Slight

Description of foliage: Dark green; small and glossy; healthy

Height and spread: 2¾ x 3¼ft (85cm x 1m)

This is a lovely repeat-flowering shrub rose that is most suited to ground-covering. It is useful for mixed plantings, containers and as a specimen on its own – if you don't mind low colour, and lots of it. If planting more than one together, space them at distances of 3¼ft (1m), to enable the stems to 'knit' together.

NAME: 'NORFOLK'

Origin: Poulsen, Denmark (1990)

Parentage: Not disclosed

USDA zone: 5

Description of bloom: Bright yellow. Double, rosette-shaped, 2in (5cm) across, carried in many large clusters

Scent: Delicate

Description of foliage: Small, glossy, mid-green; plentiful

Height and spread: 18in x 2ft (45 x 60cm)

Blooms are carried from mid-summer to late autumn. Although perfect as a ground-cover rose, it makes a good container plant as well. May be found under the name 'Poufolk'.

NAME: 'NOZOMI' AGM

Origin: Onadera, Japan (1968)

Parentage: 'Fairy Princess' x 'Sweet Fairy'

USDA zone: 6

Description of bloom: Pale blush pink, to white opening from deeper-coloured buds. Single, flat blooms 1in (2.5cm) across are carried in dense clusters, held just above the foliage

Scent: Light and musky

Description of foliage: Small, narrow, glossy, dark green but red-tinted

Height and spread: 18in x 5ft (45cm x 1.5m)

This is a very popular rose, the main attraction being the simplicity of its flowers. The low growing habit, combined with its zig-zag stems,

mean that 'Nozomi' AGM is good also for rock gardens and it seems to be at home in a Japanese-themed garden (which is perhaps not surprising when you see that the plant was raised in Japan). There is only one flowering period, which is a shame, but a bonus is that often in the autumn small red hips are produced.

NAME: 'PINK BELLS'

Origin: Poulsen, Denmark (1983)

Parentage: 'Mini Poul' x 'Temple Bells'

USDA zone: 5

Description of bloom: Clear rose-pink. Fully double, rosette carried in clusters along the lengths of the stems

Scent: Little

Description of foliage: Small, mid- to dark green, and very glossy

Height and spread: 2½ x 5ft (75cm x 1.5m)

This rose makes excellent, dense ground cover, and can be successfully trained over a low fence, or used to make fairly impenetrable hedging. Each individual flower is crammed with little petals. Despite the name, the flowers are not bell-shaped.

NAME: 'RED BLANKET'

Origin: Ilsink, Netherlands (1979)

Parentage: Seedling of 'Yesterday'

USDA zone: 6

Description of bloom: Pale crimson with a white patch towards the centre and bright yellow stamens. Semi-double

Scent: Musky and sweet; delicate

Description of foliage: Dark green

Height and spread: 3¼ x 3¼ft (1 x1m)

This is a low, loose shrub rose that is sold as a ground-cover variety but also makes a good container plant. The flowers come in clusters of 5–20, making a spectacle of colour for a long time, as it is a repeat-flowerer. Watch out for the many hundreds of small prickles though.

NAME: 'ROSY CUSHION' AGM

Origin: Interplant, Netherlands (1979)
Parentage: Seedling of 'Yesterday'
USDA zone: 6
Description of bloom: Pink with a white centre and a circle of golden stamens
Scent: Musky; delicate
Description of foliage: Dark green, always appears to be healthy
Height and spread: 3¼ x 5ft (1 x 1.5m)
One of the first purpose-bred, modern, ground-cover roses, the blooms are generally pale pink on the inside of the flower and a darker pink on the outside. It is almost constantly in flower, from early summer until mid-autumn. A dense plant, it is useful in mixed borders. 'Rosy Cushion' has masses of tiny prickles.

NAME: 'SNOW CARPET'

Origin: McGredy, New Zealand (1980)
Parentage: 'New Penny' x 'Temple Bells'
USDA zone: 5
Description of bloom: Cream at first, fading to white quickly, with a hint of yellow at the centre where the stamens are obscured by the petals folding in. Fully double
Scent: Little
Description of foliage: Clear, bright green; small, narrow, glossy
Height and spread: 15in x 4ft (38cm x 1.2m)
A very low ground-cover rose, this really does suppress weeds; its dense, matted growth overcomes all competition. When the blooms first emerge in mid-summer they seem to cover the surface of the plant. Repeat blooming is usually more profuse following a long, hot summer.

ABOVE **'Suffolk' (also sold as 'Bassino')**

NAME: 'SUFFOLK' (SYN. 'BASSINO')

Origin: Kordes, Germany (1988)
Parentage: ('Sea Foam' x Rote Max Graf) x seedling unnamed
USDA zone: 5
Description of bloom: Scarlet with occasional streaks of white, centres with packed golden stamens; single
Scent: Light and musky
Description of foliage: Light green; plentiful
Height and spread: 2½ x 5ft (75cm x 1.5m)
The blooms come in large clusters of 10–30 all over the surface of the plant. Flowers continue well into the autumn, and are usually followed by small red hips. Sold as 'Bassino' in most parts of the world, but 'Suffolk' in the UK.

NAME: 'SURREY' (SYN. 'SOMMERWIND') AGM

Origin: Kordes, Germany (1988)
Parentage: Seedling of 'The Fairy'
USDA zone: 6
Description of bloom: Dark pink fading to pale pink; double
Scent: Musky; delicate
Description of foliage: Small, semi-glossy, medium to dark green
Height and spread: 2½ x 4ft (75cm x 1.2m)
This is one of the most popular of ground-cover roses. Flowers are carried in clusters of 5–25 all over the plant's surface, making the whole plant a picture – and the individual flowers on close inspection are beautiful as well. It is a repeat-flowerer, blooming continuously from early summer to late autumn. It is also one of the few roses that go well in combination with other shrubs. Sold as 'Sommerwind' in most parts of the world, but 'Surrey' in the UK.

NAME: 'SUSSEX'

Origin: Poulsen, Denmark (1991)
Parentage: Not disclosed
USDA zone: 6
Description of bloom: Apricot-pink fading to buff at the edges; double
Scent: Light and sweet
Description of foliage: Mid- to dark green but bronzy when young; plentiful
Height and spread: 2 x 3ft (60 x 90cm)
When the buds open they are indeed apricot-pink, fading to buff, but after the first day they fade to a pink and off-white. At the same time the stamens turn from golden yellow to brown. It does not sound particularly nice, yet the flowers come in such profusion, and are so long-lasting, that the overall effect is extremely good. And, during the flowering season, there always seem to be fresh flowers to take the place of the faded ones. This rose is best in a cooler climate; for example it is much better in Denmark (its place of origin) than, say, the south of France.

NAME: 'SWANY' AGM

Origin: Meilland, France (1978)
Parentage: *Rosa sempervirens* hybrid x 'Mlle Marthe Carron'
USDA zone: 6
Description of bloom: White; double
Scent: Musky; delicate
Description of foliage: Dark, small, glossy; one of the few evergreen roses
Height and spread: 2 x 5ft (60cm x 1.5m)
Very useful for places where greenery in winter is wanted. It was the first ground-cover rose from the Meilland stable, and is one of the best. It has a loose, lax habit, making it useful for scrambling over banks, or even old tree stumps. The white flowers have the palest of pink tinges as they open.

MINIATURE AND PATIO ROSES

Miniature roses were first bred for outdoors, and this is where the hardier forms are most 'at home'. However, generally, they are now raised for growing indoors, and today you will see benches of these plants at garden centres, for sale as indoor plants.

They have a certain charm and bring a little taste of rose growing to those whose garden may be no more than a windowsill. But, to my mind, these roses do also have a place in the garden.

Miniature roses are best sited near to a patio, perhaps where you can see them at close quarters while enjoying a cool drink on a warm, sunny afternoon.

The small, hardy, bush roses that have the generic label of 'patio rose' are seen to advantage in a similar setting. These are quite an indistinct category, being larger than miniatures and smaller than hybrid teas and floribundas, but they can have the same habits and shapes as hybrid teas and floribundas.

ABOVE 'Angela Rippon'

NAME: 'ANGELA RIPPON'
Origin: De Ruiter, The Netherlands (1978)
Parentage: 'Rosy Jewel' x 'Zorina'
USDA zone: 6
Description of bloom: Salmon pink; fully double
Scent: Light
Description of foliage: Dark green; small and provided in good number
Height and spread: 18 x 12in (45 x 30cm)
This is a true miniature rose, named after the famous British television newsreader from the 1970s and 80s. This rose is excellent for containers, windowboxes and group plantings in a raised bed, or front of a border. It flowers throughout summer and autumn, each bloom being some 1½in (4cm) across, opens flat from an original 'urn' shape.

NAME: 'ANNA FORD' AGM
Origin: Harkness, UK (1980)
Parentage: 'Southampton' x 'Darling Flame'
USDA zone: 6
Description of bloom: Bright orange; semi-double
Scent: Light and sweet
Description of foliage: Rich medium green; small in size and shiny
Height and spread: 2 x 2ft (60 x 60cm)

Named after another famous British television newsreader from the 1970s and 80s, this was one of the first patio roses. The flowers are an intense rose-orange, with a yellow patch towards the centre. The blooms turn to red and pink as they age, and are followed in autumn by small, pale orange, tomato-shaped hips.

NAME: 'BABY MASQUERADE'

Origin: Tantau, Germany (1955)
Parentage: 'Tom Thumb' or 'Peon' x 'Masquerade'
USDA zone: 6
Description of bloom: Opening yellow, becoming pink, ending dark crimson; double
Scent: Little
Description of foliage: Very small, dark green and plentiful
Height and spread: 10 x 16in (25 x 40cm)
This old variety remains popular today, in the main because of its variable flower colourings that are so typical of its parent, 'Masquerade'. To add to the kaleidoscope of colours, the petal backs are always paler, and the outer petals are more intensely shaded than the inner ones. It is a very floriferous plant throughout summer and early autumn.

NAME: 'BLUE PETER'

Origin: De Ruiter, The Netherlands (1982)
Parentage: 'Little Flirt' x seedling
USDA zone: 6
Description of bloom: Lavender-purple; double
Scent: Light and delicate
Description of foliage: Light green; small, glossy and plentiful
Height and spread: 15 x 12in (38 x 30cm)
This miniature bush rose flowers throughout summer and until the middle of autumn. Recommended for small, confined spaces, and for containers. May also be found under the name 'Ruiblun'.

ABOVE 'Anna Ford' AGM

ABOVE 'Blue Peter'

NAME: 'BOYS' BRIGADE'

Origin: Cocker, UK (1983)
Parentage: 'Darling Flame' x ('Little Flirt' x 'Marlena')
USDA zone: 6
Description of bloom: Dark red, cream-white centred; single
Scent: Slight
Description of foliage: Small in size, olive green and glossy
Height and spread: 18 x 18in (45 x 45cm)
A lovely patio rose with large clusters of small, bright, dark-red flowers, each with a creamy white eye. It produces dense, bushy growths, and flowers continuously until mid-autumn. May also be found under the name 'Cockdinkum'.

NAME: 'BRIGHT SMILE'

Origin: Dickson, Northern Ireland (1980)
Parentage: 'Eurorose' seedling
USDA zone: 6
Description of bloom: Butter-yellow, richer in the centre; flat, semi-double
Scent: Light, sweet and fruity
Description of foliage: Bright green, glossy and frequently with faint flushes of red; medium-sized
Height and spread: 2ft x 18in (60 x 45cm)
Each flower of this patio rose is a bright mid-yellow, deeper towards the centre, and when it opens you can see the boss of central golden stamens. It has a long flowering season, and is relatively weather-resistant, not minding long days, intense sunlight, or prolonged periods of rain. Suitable for low hedging.

NAME: 'CIDER CUP' AGM

Origin: Dickson, Northern Ireland (1987)
Parentage: 'Memento' x ('Liverpool Echo' x 'Woman's Own')
USDA zone: 6
Description of bloom: Deep apricot-pink; double, with a golden-yellow boss of stamens.
Scent: Delicate and fruity
Description of foliage: Dark green; small in size and glossy

Height and spread: 2½ x 2ft (75 x 60cm)
The buds of this patio rose make wonderful buttonholes, and when the blooms open out they make a brilliant splash of bright colour. The colouring pales towards the edges of the petals. The flowers are produced in clusters of 5–10, from mid-summer until late autumn.

NAME: 'DRESDEN DOLL'

Origin: Moore, US (1975)
Parentage: 'Fairy Moss' seedling
USDA zone: 6
Description of bloom: Rose-pink; double
Scent: Light and sweet
Description of foliage: Mid-green, medium-sized leaves
Height and spread: 16 x 12in (40 x 30cm)
This is a miniature 'moss' rose. Moss roses are so-called because they have a green or brown 'moss', made up from hundreds of sticky hairs on the flowers' stalks, which lead right up to the bases of the flowers. Curiously, this moss is often pine-scented (as is the case here). The full head of petals of 'Dresden Doll' open out to reveal a centre of tiny yellow stamens. It repeat-flowers well, and is best grown close to patios and other places where the flowers and conspicuous stalks can be seen at close quarters. This variety is susceptible to mildew; it therefore enjoys hotter summers and so thrives better in warmer climates.

NAME: 'FESTIVAL'

Origin: Kordes, Germany (1994)
Parentage: Regensberg seedling
USDA zone: 6
Description of bloom: Rich, velvety, scarlet-crimson with a paler petal reverse and irregular white markings; double
Scent: Light
Description of foliage: Dark bluish-green, sometimes with crimson edges edges; small and glossy
Height and spread: 2½ft x 20in (75 x 50cm)
The striking flowers of this miniature rose,

ABOVE **'Festival'**

combined with the small, compact habit of the plant, make it very useful for the smaller garden. Flowers come in small clusters of 3–5, and occasionally singly. Good for containers or the front of a border, but beware of the prickles.

NAME: **'GENTLE TOUCH'**

Origin: Dickson, Northern Ireland (1986)
Parentage: 'Memento' x ('Liverpool Echo' x 'Woman's Own')
USDA zone: 6
Description of bloom: Pale pink; double
Scent: Light and musky

Description of foliage: Dark green; small, glossy and plentiful
Height and spread: 20 x 16in (50 x 40cm)
It is surprising that this plant is so different from 'Cider Cup', since it has exactly the same parentage. 'Gentle Touch' is a delightful patio rose with dainty, pale-pink blooms and a hint of salmon pink on the upper parts of the petals. The blooms start out as perfect little buds which are ideal as buttonholes. They open out to flat rosettes, fully exposing the central golden stamens. It repeat-flowers well.

NAME: 'PRETTY POLLY' (SYN. 'PINK SYMPHONIE') AGM

Origin: Meilland, France (1987)
Parentage: Parentage not disclosed
USDA zone: 6
Description of bloom: Clear rose-pink; double.
Scent: Light and musky
Description of foliage: Mid-green; small, plentiful and glossy
Height and spread: 16 x 18in (40 x 45cm)
This rose, a winner of many professional rose trials, can be thought of as either a miniature or a patio rose. Its petals are a darker pink on the reverse, and this almost gives it a two-tone effect, but in clear rose-pink. The blooms come in clusters, well spaced all over the plant. It makes a wonderful container rose.

NAME: 'QUEEN MOTHER' AGM

Origin: Kordes, Germany (1991)
Parentage: *R. wichurana* seedling x 'Toynbee Hall'
USDA zone: 5
Description of bloom: Clear pink; semi-double
Scent: Delicate
Description of foliage: Mid-green, small in size and glossy
Height and spread: 2 x 2½ft (60 x 75cm)
A patio rose with style, this was for several years the most widely sold rose in England. It was named, of course, in honour of Queen Elizabeth, the mother of Queen Elizabeth II, to celebrate her 90th birthday in 1990. The blooms seem to have a slightly deeper colour in cooler weather. They open out quite flat, making

ABOVE 'Pretty Polly' AGM

the central boss of stamens – which are of varying lengths – highly visible. The flowers come in great profusion until late autumn. It well deserves its popularity.

NAME: 'RED ACE'

Origin: De Ruiter, The Netherlands (1982)
Parentage: 'Scarletta' x seedling
USDA zone: 6
Description of bloom: Rich, deep crimson; semi-double
Scent: Slight
Description of foliage: Dark green; small in size and plentiful
Height and spread: 12 x 12in (30 x 30cm)
This miniature rose has a tremendously long flowering period, from the last spring frosts practically until the first autumn frosts. Its size makes it appropriate for container growing, even in small containers such as windowboxes. It is a very fine rose, and one of the richest of the reds.

NAME: 'SWEET DREAM' AGM

Origin: Fryer, UK (1988)
Parentage: seedling x ('Anytime' x 'Liverpool Echo') x ('New Penny' x seedling)
USDA zone: 6
Description of bloom: Peach-apricot, fading to buff; fully double
Scent: Good, sweet and fruity
Description of foliage: Dark green; small in size and matt
Height and spread: 2½ft x 18in (75 x 45cm)
A best-selling patio rose ever since its introduction, when it was named 'Rose of the Year'. The colour combines well with most other flower colours, so this rose goes well with most plants. 'Sweet Dream' repeat-flowers well into autumn, and has quite a delicious scent. The flowers are very cupped and are produced in congested clusters of 5–15 individual blooms.

ABOVE **'Red Ace'**

NAME: 'SWEET MAGIC' AGM

Origin: Dickson, Northern Ireland (1986)
Parentage: 'Peek-a-Boo' x 'Bright Smile'
USDA zone: 6
Description of bloom: Golden orange, flushed with pink; double
Scent: Moderate and sweet
Description of foliage: Mid-green; small, healthy and glossy
Height and spread: 2 x 2ft (60 x 60cm)
'Sweet Magic' is a popular miniature rose, ▶

with a more regular flower shape than most other small roses. Bright golden orange flowers, later fade to pink, but the regular shape of the bloom is maintained, making it a very appealing rose over a long flowering period. A compact plant, with leaves fully in proportion to the flowers. Blackspot disease may be a problem, however.

NAME: 'TOP MARKS'

Origin: Fryer, UK (1992)
Parentage: ('Anytime' x 'Liverpool Echo') x ('New Penny' x seedling) x seedling
USDA zone: 6
Description of bloom: Bright orange-vermillion; fully double
Scent: Light and musky
Description of foliage: Mid-green; small in size and glossy
Height and spread: 16 x 18in (40 x 45cm)

A patio rose that keeps its colour well, 'Top Marks' makes a dense, compact bush but has very prickly stems. The blooms come in clusters of 3–15. It can be prone to blackspot disease.

NAME: 'WHITE PET' (SYN. 'LITTLE WHITE PET') AGM

Origin: Henderson, US (1879)
Parentage: Sport of 'Félicité et Perpétue'
USDA zone: 5
Description of bloom: White, pink in bud; fully double pompon-shaped
Scent: Sweet and delicate
Description of foliage: Bluish green; small, plentiful and evergreen
Height and spread: 2 x 2ft (60 x 60cm)
This is another of the rare evergreen roses. 'White Pet' is a dwarf rose – i.e. neither truly a miniature nor a patio rose, as it was grown well

ABOVE 'White Pet' AGM

ABOVE **Miniature roses are frequently sold in garden centres as house plants – indeed, in the background of this picture, taken in a shop, you can see African violet indoor plants.**

before these terms were in common use – with a fascinating history. In 1879, Peter Henderson, a florist in New York, found a dwarf, repeat-flowering natural sport of the climbing rose 'Félicité et Perpétue'. The flowers and foliage were identical, but the habit was tiny compared to the typical 16ft (5m) stems frequently made by the original climber. He selected and grew it and introduced it to an appreciative market of gardeners, and it remains until this day, some 130 years later. The plant tolerates partial shade, repeat-flowers well and has a charming fragrance. Its main weakness, which it shares with its original plant, is that the blooms tend to stay in place on the plant until they are completely brown, after which they will drop. This can make the plant appear untidy towards the latter half of the flowering season.

NAME: 'YELLOW DOLL'

Origin: Moore, US (1962)
Parentage: 'Golden Glow' x 'Zee'
USDA zone: 5
Description of bloom: Primrose yellow, with golden-yellow stamens; semi-double
Scent: Fruity but delicate
Description of foliage: Dark green; glossy
Height and spread: 16 x 12in (40 x 30cm)

One of the parents of this miniature rose is 'Golden Glow', a rambler rose of acknowledged hardiness. This makes 'Yellow Doll' a very hardy offspring. The blooms open from pointed buds, eventually revealing the central cluster of golden-yellow stamens. The primrose colour fades to cream, especially at the edges of the petals. It is a neat, compact plant but, in its own way, fairly sturdy and vigorous.

HYBRID TEA ROSES

For a while in the 1980s, botanists and world rose authorities tried to change the names 'hybrid tea' and 'floribunda', as they felt these terms did not adequately represent the technical qualities of the roses. Instead of 'hybrid tea' they suggested the term 'large-flowered bush rose'. This, they said, was exactly what these roses were. The public, however, disliked the suggestion, and I am delighted to say that hybrid tea roses are so-called to this day.

The name derives from the fact that these roses are hybrids of the original tea roses, which were themselves thought to smell faintly of tea.

A second theory, which can neither be proved nor disproved, is that tea roses came over to the UK from China (where they were native) on the tea ships of the East India Company.

There is a degree of snobbery about roses, and many rose purists do not consider hybrid teas worthy of garden space. This is a shame, for the large and often spectacular blooms – held, in the main singly, on short stems – can be a real joy; they are also some of the most strongly scented roses of all. They are spectacular plants and any garden containing roses should have one or two – at the very least.

ABOVE 'Alexander' AGM

NAME: 'ALEXANDER' AGM

Origin: Harkness, UK (1972)
Parentage: 'Super Star' x ('Ann Elizabeth' x 'Allgold')
USDA zone: 6
Description of bloom: Red-vermillion
Scent: Delicate
Description of foliage: Dark green; glossy and carried in quantity
Height and spread: 6½ x 4ft (2 x 1.2m)
This is arguably the most vividly coloured rose of all time. However, it is also one of the most vigorous of hybrid tea roses, and can, if not controlled, quickly outgrow its space. The flowers are usually carried singly during the first flush, and in later flushes they are in clusters of 3–7. It is excessively prickly, and susceptible to mildew and blackspot. On the plus side it is free-flowering and rain-resistant.

NAME: 'BEAUTY STAR'

Origin: Fryer, UK (1990)
Parentage: 'Corso' x seedling
USDA zone: 6
Description of bloom: Orange, with paler silvery reverse to the petals
Scent: Strong and fruity

Description of foliage: Mid-green, glossy
Height and spread: 5 x 3¼ft (1.5 x 1m)
This rose enjoys warmer weather, in which it grows more vigorously and is more floriferous. The orange flowers are darker in cool weather, and pinker in warmer climates. They are generally carried singly on long stems, but sometimes they are held in small, well-spaced clusters. It is extremely prickly, and in cool climates is prone to mildew.

NAME: 'BELLE EPOQUE'

Origin: Fryer, UK (1994)
Parentage: 'Remember Me' x 'Helmut Schmidt'
USDA zone: 6
Description of bloom: Pale bronze-yellow
Scent: Light and fruity
Description of foliage: Bright green; healthy-looking and tough
Height and spread: 5 x 3¼ft (1.5 x 1m)
The blooms are pale bronze-yellow, but on the reverse of the petals the hues are darker, almost orange with suggestions of pink and russet-brown. This is an unusual combination for a

ABOVE **'Beauty Star'**

hybrid tea, which makes this variety rather special. The flower buds are elegant in their own right, eventually opening into lightly cupped flowers. It is an excellent, repeat-flowering variety.

ABOVE **'Belle Epoque'**

ABOVE 'Blue Moon'

ABOVE 'Christian Dior'

NAME: 'BLUE MOON' (SYN. 'MAINZER FASTNACHT')

Origin: Tantau, Germany (1964)
Parentage: seedling of 'Sterling Silver' x seedling
USDA zone: 6
Description of bloom: Lilac-mauve, tinted blue in warm weather
Scent: Strong and sweet
Description of foliage: Mid-green; large in size and glossy
Height and spread: 3 x 2ft (90 x 60cm)

This is almost certainly the best-known and most widely grown of the so-called 'blue roses'. In reality blue is a colour that has so far eluded the rose-breeding fraternity. They are getting closer, however, and in the 1960s when this variety first came on the market it caused a sensation. Other, better blues have been produced since, but this was the 'original', and in many ways its tones are unique and quite adorable. The blooms open slowly from large, elegant buds, and expand into the most exquisite rose shape. Although perfectly hardy in most temperate climates, it does tend to perform best in the warmer countries.

NAME: 'CHRISTIAN DIOR'

Origin: Meilland, France (1958)
Parentage: 'Mme A. Meilland' x 'Rouge Meilland'
USDA zone: 6
Description of bloom: Scarlet to dark crimson
Scent: Light and fruity
Description of foliage: Dark green, copper-coloured at first; glossy
Height and spread: 5 x 4ft (1.5 x 1.2m)

The flowers of this variety are large, full and classically shaped. When fully open they fade slightly, taking on more of the scarlet shades. Sometimes there are a few white stripes which appear from the centre of the flower along the lengths of the petals.

ABOVE **'Claret'**

NAME: **'CLARET'**

Origin: Fryer, UK (2005)
Parentage: Not disclosed
USDA zone: 6
Description of bloom: Dark red
Scent: Strong
Description of foliage: Medium green; semi-glossy, medium-sized leaves
Height and spread: 3 x 2½ft (90 x 75cm)
The rich, deep-red flowers are carried from late spring until the first frosts of autumn. It is an ideal rose for borders, mixed plantings, large and small beds. If planting more than one, set them 2ft (60cm) apart.

NAME: **'DOUBLE DELIGHT'**

Origin: Swim & Ellis, US (1977)
Parentage: 'Granada' x 'Garden Party'
USDA zone: 5
Description of bloom: Cream-white and bright crimson
Scent: Very strong; fruity and sweet
Description of foliage: Mid-green; matt, and carried in quantity

ABOVE **'Double Delight'**

Height and spread: 3¼ x 2½ft (1m x 75cm)
The name of this rose may refer to the dual tone colours of the flowers, or the fact that it offers a 'double delight' in terms of flower colour and scent. The blooms of this variety are creamy-white at first, with just a tinge of red on the outer petals. As they age, however, the crimson colouring ▶

of the 'Double Delight' blooms spreads, especially in hot weather. This results in a stunning contrast between the cream-white hearts and the layers of bright crimson outer petals. Interestingly, if you grow this variety in a greenhouse, as has been tried by nurserymen for the cut flower industry, the flowers – somewhat surprisingly – are white. This is because the natural red colourings in 'Double Delight' are created by the action of ultraviolet light on the natural pigments in the petals but, within a greenhouse, the glass filters out the ultraviolet light.

ABOVE 'Dutch Gold'

NAME: 'DUTCH GOLD'

Origin: Wisbech Plant Co., UK (1978)
Parentage: 'Peer Gynt' x 'Whisky Mac'
USDA zone: 6
Description of bloom: Rich golden yellow
Scent: Strong and sweet
Description of foliage: Dark green; large in size in size and matt
Height and spread: 3¼ x 2½ft (1m x 75cm)
One of the best of the pure yellow roses, the blooms of 'Dutch Gold' are fully double and some 6in (15cm) across. It has a strong scent and the plant offers good disease resistance.

NAME: 'ENA HARKNESS'

Origin: Norman, UK (1946)
Parentage: 'Crimson Glory' x 'Southport'
USDA zone: 6
Description of bloom: Deep scarlet-crimson
Scent: Sweet and strong
Description of foliage: Mid-green, matt and somewhat sparse
Height and spread: 2½ x 2ft (75 x 60cm)
Although bred by an amateur rose breeder (Englishman Albert Norman), this rose was bought and introduced by the Harkness rose nursery, and quickly put the family name on the rose map. The Harkness family now run one of England's largest and most prestigious rose nurseries. This is a great rose, with superb colouring, and good resistance to rainfall. It is also highly floriferous, with a long flowering season – practically into late autumn. Its main disadvantage is that it has a weakish stalk, which means that the flowers, particularly the larger ones, have a tendency to droop.

NAME: 'FRAGRANT CLOUD' (SYN. 'DUFTWOLKE')

Origin: Tantau, Germany (1967)
Parentage: seedling x 'Prima Ballerina'
USDA zone: 5
Description of bloom: Coral red, aging through to dusky scarlet, to purple-red
Scent: Very strong; sweet and fruity

Description of foliage: Dark green, large and leathery

Height and spread: 5 x 3¼ft (1.5 x 1m)

My late father, who was a far more knowledgeable and better rosarian than ever I could be, went on record numerous times saying that this rose was his favourite. It is not hard to see why. It has beauty in form, its colouring makes a stunning statement, and it gives off one of the most powerful of any scent in the garden. It is also a strong and vigorous grower, is relatively disease-resistant and, in addition, it flowers almost continuously and well into autumn. Its colouring is not really found in any other rose, particularly the purplish tints when the blooms start to fade.

NAME: 'FREEDOM' AGM

Origin: Dickson, Northern Ireland (1984)
Parentage: ('Eurorose' x 'Taifun') x 'Bright Smile'
USDA zone: 6
Description of bloom: Clear, bright yellow
Scent: Light and sweet ▶

ABOVE **'Fragrant Cloud'**

ABOVE **'Freedom' AGM**

Description of foliage: Mid-green; glossy and carried in quantity

Height and spread: 2½ x 2ft (75 x 60cm)

The yellow colour remains throughout the life of the flower, with only minimal fading. Blooms are usually borne singly on long, thick, upright stems. It is a handsome, classic-looking hybrid tea.

NAME: 'GRANDPA DICKSON'

Origin: Dickson, Northern Ireland (1966)

Parentage: ('Kordes Perfecta' x 'Governador Braga da Cruz') x 'Harry Wheatcroft'

USDA zone: 6

Description of bloom: Pale yellow, flushing pink in warm weather

Scent: Delicate

Description of foliage: Pale to mid-green; glossy and sparse

Height and spread: 4 x 3ft (1.2m x 90cm)

Named after Alexander Dickson, for many years the head of the Dickson family of rose nurserymen in the Ulster region of Northern Ireland. In the US, and other parts of the world, this variety is more than likely to be found under the name 'Irish Gold'. Both the buds and the open flowers of this rose are very elegantly shaped. It repeat-flowers well but it is not very vigorous and is prone to blackspot.

ABOVE *'Henri Matisse'*

NAME: 'HENRI MATISSE'

Origin: Delbard, France (1995)
Parentage: ('Lara' x 'Candia') x seedling
USDA zone: 6
Description of bloom: Crimson, with irregular pale pink markings
Scent: Light
Description of foliage: Bright medium green; healthy and glossy
Height and spread: 5 x 3ft (1.5m x 90cm)

Although many rose purists disagree with me, I feel there are too few bi-coloured roses. The bi-colour forms seem to be loathed and loved in equal measure. 'Henri Matisse' is a very good one. The deep crimson flowers are marked by as much as 25 per cent of the surface area with pale pink which, to my eye, makes for a very pleasing effect. For a short period after the rose's introduction, it was grown commercially under glass for cut-flower production, because the flowers are carried on relatively long stems, which are ideal for cutting. However, it was quickly dropped by many of the growers, as it does not produce enough volume of flower for the 'cut and thrust' of the commercial cut-flower markets. This doesn't detract from it, as it is an excellent garden plant.

NAME: 'ICE CREAM' (SYN. 'MEMOIRE') AGM

Origin: Kordes, Germany (1992)
Parentage: Not disclosed
USDA zone: 6
Description of bloom: White, very faintly flushed lemon yellow
Scent: Strong and sweet
Description of foliage: Dark green, copper-red in the early stages
Height and spread: 4 x 2½ft (1.2m x 75cm)

This is one of the few roses that confuse gardeners, both amateur and professional. On the one hand it is a hybrid tea because of its flower size – up to 6in (15cm) across – and on the other it is a floribunda, because the blooms usually come in clusters. Such roses are

ABOVE **'Ice Cream' AGM**

frequently termed 'intermediate'. Because of the impact of the individual blooms, I always list it as a hybrid tea, but not all nurserymen agree. Regardless of this, it is a fabulous plant, and one of the best roses to be introduced within the past 30 years. As with many roses with a strong scent, it is at its most powerful when the flowers are half open.

NAME: 'INGRID BERGMAN' AGM

Origin: Poulsen, Denmark (1984)
Parentage: 'Precious Platinum' x seedling
USDA zone: 5
Description of bloom: Pure dark red; no markings or particularly visible stamens
Scent: Medium strength; sweet
Description of foliage: Dark green; glossy and leathery, crimson when young
Height and spread: 2½ x 2½ft (75 x 75cm)▶

ABOVE **'Ingrid Bergman' AGM**

BELOW **'Just Joey' AGM**

Named after the popular Hollywood actress, the deep red flowers of 'Ingrid Bergman' open from long, elegant buds that are almost black. They are fully double and stand up well to the rain.

NAME: **'JUST JOEY' AGM**

Origin: Cants, UK (1972)
Parentage: 'Fragrant Cloud' x 'Dr A.J. Verhag'
USDA zone: 6
Description of bloom: Coppery-fawn, with buff-pink tints
Scent: Medium strength; sweet
Description of foliage: Dark green; leathery, sparse
Height and spread: 3 x 2½ft (90 x 75cm)
The flowers are large, and of a colour that is quite unusual. The stamens are crimson, not the usual yellow for roses, which adds to its charm. It does best in a cooler climate, where its colours and scent are more intense.

NAME: 'LOVING MEMORY' (SYN. 'BURGUND 81')

Origin: Kordes, Germany (1981)
Parentage: 'Henkell Royal' x seedling
USDA zone: 6
Description of bloom: Deep, bright red-crimson
Scent: Slight
Description of foliage: Deep green; large
Height and spread: 5 x 2½ft (1.5m x 75cm)

Before the flowers open, the buds are almost black. When open, the outer petals are dark crimson, whereas the inner petals are a brighter red. As the flower ages it tends to lose its shape, so that there is a formless mass of petals. For all of this, the colouring is so strong, it makes this rose a very worthy garden plant.

NAME: 'NATIONAL TRUST'

Origin: McGredy, Northern Ireland (1970)
Parentage: 'Evelyn Fison' x 'King of Hearts'
USDA zone: 6
Description of bloom: Scarlet-crimson
Scent: Light and sweet
Description of foliage: Dark green and red-tinted; plentiful and matt
Height and spread: 3 x 2ft (90 x 60cm)

The outer petals of this rose fold back to a point, giving a spiky effect, contrasting with the rounded whorls of the inner petals as they open. The petals are quite thick, making them stand up well to the rain, and they don't seem to fade as they age. Flowers are carried well into autumn. Some of the blooms can develop a split centre (where two 'hearts' are formed), which makes this a poor rose for exhibiting, but it is still a good garden plant.

ABOVE RIGHT 'Loving Memory'

RIGHT 'National Trust'

ABOVE **'Peace' AGM**

NAME: 'PEACE' (SYN. 'MME A. MEILLAND') AGM

Origin: Meilland, France (1942)
Parentage: 'Joanna Hill' x ('Charles P. Kilham' x 'Margaret McGredy')
USDA zone: 6
Description of bloom: Pale yellow with a crimson edge, fading to cream and pink
Scent: Medium strength; sweet
Description of foliage: Bright green; large, glossy and plentiful
Height and spread: 5 x 4ft (1.5 x 1.2m)
Originally named 'Mme A. Meilland', this rose first came to prominence just as the Second World War ended, so it was marketed under the name of 'Peace'. Gardeners liked it for its garden qualities, just as much as for its symbolic name. It has since become, probably, the world's most famous rose. The flowers are large, often 5½in (14cm) across, and are beautiful at every stage of their development. The colours of the flowers do tend to vary slightly from season to season, and from garden to garden. The scent, too, is variable; some maintain that it is strong and powerful, whilst others reckon it to be scentless. Part of its charm is that you never quite know what you will get, and it is also reasonably disease-resistant. A number of sports have been created and marketed from this rose, and these include 'Chicago Peace' (rather more pink), 'Climbing Peace' (same flower colouring as 'Peace', but on a climber) and 'Kronenburg' (dark, velvety-red on the upper petal surfaces, pure yellow on the reverse).

NAME: 'REMEMBER ME' AGM

Origin: Cocker, UK (1984)
Parentage: 'Ann Letts' x ('Dainty Maid' x 'Pink Favorite')
USDA zone: 6
Description of bloom: Deep copper-orange
Scent: Rich and fruity
Description of foliage: Dark green; small glossy and abundant
Height and spread: 4 x 3ft (1.2m x 90cm)
A close look at the flowers of this rose will show you not just copper-orange, but a host of other shades. The buds are generally this colour and they open to a shade of dark

peach, but there are hints of yellow and brown, cream and beige, fawn and tan, and even salmon pink. It is a tight and compact rose, and quite prickly.

NAME: 'ROTARY SUNRISE'

Origin: Fryer, UK (2004)
Parentage: Not disclosed
USDA zone: 6
Description of bloom: Blend of yellows
Scent: Medium strength; musky
Description of foliage: Olive green; medium-sized and matt
Height and spread: 3 x 2½ft (90 x 75cm)
The yellow flowers are carried from late spring until the first frosts of autumn. It is an ideal variety for borders, mixed plantings, large and small beds. If planting more than one, set them 2ft (60cm) apart.

ABOVE **'Remember Me' AGM**

ABOVE **'Rotary Sunrise'**

ABOVE 'Royal William' AGM

NAME: 'ROYAL WILLIAM' (SYN. 'DUFTZAUBER 84') AGM

Origin: Kordes, Germany (1984)
Parentage: seedling of 'Feuerzauber'
USDA zone: 6
Description of bloom: Deep crimson
Scent: Strong, sweet and fruity
Description of foliage: Dark green; semi-glossy and large
Height and spread: 4 x 3ft (1.2m x 90cm)
Few things in nature can be regarded as faultless, but many experts say that this is the perfect rose: the exquisite large flowers have a beautiful, unfading quality, with the tips of the petals sometimes slightly darker than the rest; it is an excellent garden rose, is good for cutting, and it has a delicious scent. It also repeat-flowers well.

NAME: 'SAVOY HOTEL' AGM

Origin: Harkness, UK (1987)
Parentage: 'Silver Jubilee' x 'Amber Queen'
USDA zone: 6
Description of bloom: Light pink
Scent: Medium strength; sweet
Description of foliage: Dark green; semi-glossy and plentiful
Height and spread: 3 x 2½ft (90 x 75cm)
Named to commemorate the centenary of the famous London hotel, the pale-pink petals of this rose have raspberry-pink reverses. Much of the flower's beauty comes from the shades and tones reflected in the folds of the petals. The blooms are held on long stems, which make them good for cutting.

ABOVE 'Savoy Hotel' AGM

NAME: 'SILVER JUBILEE' AGM

Origin: Cocker, UK (1978)
Parentage: (['Highlight' x 'Königin der Rosen'] x ['Parkdirektor Riggers' x 'Harry Wheatcroft']) x 'Mischief'
USDA zone: 6
Description of bloom: Shades of dark pink and with a hint of apricot
Scent: Light and sweet
Description of foliage: Dark green; large in size and glossy
Height and spread: 3 x 2½ft (90 x 75cm)

'Silver Jubilee' was named in honour of the 25th anniversary of the accession to the throne by Queen Elizabeth II, and it is an extraordinarily fine rose. The outer petals are dark pink, and the inner ones are lighter, and there seem to be shades of apricot in between. As with most hybrid tea roses, the blooms generally come singly, but they will sometimes come in clusters of up to five. It is generally trouble-free, but can sometimes be prone to blackspot.

ABOVE 'Silver Jubilee' AGM

ABOVE 'Special Occasion'

ABOVE 'Tequila Sunrise' AGM

NAME: 'SPECIAL OCCASION'

Origin: Fryer, UK (1995)
Parentage: Not disclosed
USDA zone: 6
Description of bloom: Apricot
Scent: Medium strength; sweet and fruity
Description of foliage: Dark green; glossy
Height and spread: 4 x 2½ft (1.2m x 75cm)
This is one of the first hybrid teas to flower in the year, and it repeats frequently, right until the end of the growing season. Its apricot petals are paler at the edges, and darker towards the centre. Shadows of copper-pink appear between the petals.

NAME: 'TEQUILA SUNRISE' AGM

Origin: Dickson, Northern Ireland (1988)
Parentage: 'Bonfire Night' x 'Freedom'
USDA zone: 6
Description of bloom: Golden-yellow, with scarlet edges to the petals
Scent: Light and fruity
Description of foliage: Mid-green and glossy
Height and spread: 5 x 4ft (1.5 x 1.2m)

Anyone who knows the cocktail of the same name will instantly recognize the colouring. Blooms open to a deep yellow, but quickly pick up a bright red edging to the petals, which expands as the bloom ages. A bush in full flower is a dazzling array of yellows and reds.

NAME: 'VELVET FRAGRANCE'

Origin: Fryer, UK (1988)
Parentage: 'Mildred Scheel' x 'Fragrant Cloud'
USDA zone: 6
Description of bloom: Crimson
Scent: Sweet; very strong
Description of foliage: Dark green; semi-glossy and large
Height and spread: 5½ x 4ft (1.75 x 1.2m)
This rose prefers hot, dry weather, which brings out the best of the crimson colouring. The petals definitely have a velvety sheen over them, so it is not difficult to see how the rose was named, and its powerful scent can fill a small garden on a still evening. Flowers keep coming until late autumn. Emerging shoots have a coppery tinge, but the leaves are susceptible to blackspot.

NAME: 'YORKSHIRE BANK' (SYN. 'TRUE LOVE')

Origin: De Ruiter, The Netherlands (1979)
Parentage: 'Pascali' x 'Peer Gynt'
USDA zone: 6
Description of bloom: Cream-white, with buff, pale yellow and pink
Scent: Medium-strength; sweet
Description of foliage: Dark green; healthy-looking and plentiful
Height and spread: 4 x 2½ft (1.2m x 75cm)
An extremely popular rose throughout Europe, the flowers usually come singly, but occasionally in small clusters, up to five. It is usually pruned hard each year, in the normal style for hybrid teas; but if left, it will develop into a good-sized bushy shrub rose, that will be covered with many – smaller – blooms.

ABOVE 'Velvet Fragrance'

ABOVE 'Yorkshire Bank'

OTHER HYBRID TEA ROSES WORTHY OF NOTE:

There are, actually, several hundred other hybrid tea roses that make excellent additions to the rose garden. Obviously we do not have the space to describe them all here, but the following are well worth considering:

'**Alec's Red**': Deep crimson to rich cherry red.
'**Apricot Silk**': A blend of pink, apricot and peach shades.

'**A Whiter Shade of Pale**': White with the merest hint of yellow.
'**Bettina**': Bright orange.
'**Blessings**' AGM: A blend of pinks, apricots and salmons.
'**Buccaneer**': Buttercup yellow.
'**Chandos Beauty**': Blend of soft pinks.
'**Cheshire Life**': Vermilion orange.
'**City of Gloucester**': Saffron yellow, shaded gold.
'**Doris Tysterman**': Rich coppery orange.

ABOVE '**A Whiter Shade of Pale**'

ABOVE '**Chandos Beauty**'

ABOVE '**City of Gloucester**'

ABOVE '**Julia's Rose**'

'Ernest H. Morse': Rich, deep red.

'Harry Wheatcroft': Scarlet, with clearly defined yellow stripes (also sold as 'Picadilly').

'Julia's Rose': Copper-bronze with distinct brown-pink tints.

'King's Macc': An attractive blend of apricot, gold and cream.

'King's Ransom': Golden yellow, unfading.

'Mischief': Coral salmon.

'Mullard Jubilee': Deep rose pink.

'Pascali': White-shaded cream.

'Peer Gynt': Canary yellow flushed pink.

'Polar Star': White.

'Princess Royal': Golden apricot.

'Ruby Wedding': Clear dark ruby-crimson.

'Super Star': Vermillion to pale scarlet.

'Terracotta': Blend of tan and rust shades.

'Troika' AGM: Orange-bronze, shaded red.

'Wendy Cussons': Cherry pink to pink.

'Whisky Mac': Golden amber and orange.

ABOVE **'King's Macc'**

ABOVE **'Princess Royal'**

ABOVE **'Ruby Wedding'**

ABOVE **'Terracotta'**

FLORIBUNDA ROSES

Whereas a hybrid tea bears its flowers singly on stems, a floribunda carries them in clusters, or trusses, and several blooms open at one time in each truss.

Before the early 1900s there was no such thing as a floribunda rose, but just before the start of the First World War these hybrids were starting to be bred, in the main between hybrid teas and polyantha shrub roses. The Poulsen family from Denmark were responsible for the development of these early varieties.

It was not until the 1950s, however, that the name floribunda was used to describe this new race of roses. Now, the floribunda is an essential part of any rose garden.

No other type of rose offers so many blooms, in so many colours, for such a long flowering period, in return for relatively little in the way of care and maintenance. Individually, the flower from a floribunda may not be as perfectly formed as that of a hybrid tea, but the floribundas make up for this by providing an unrivalled amount of colour, along with reliability and a long flowering season.

Finally, many experienced rose growers have said that floribundas do not have the range of perfumes that other roses have, but I disagree. It may be true that hybrid teas, in total, are more scented, but there are quite a few floribundas that can compete when it comes to fragrance.

ABOVE 'Amber Queen' AGM

NAME: 'AMBER QUEEN' AGM

Origin: Harkness, UK (1983)
Parentage: 'Southampton' x 'Typhoon'
USDA zone: 6
Description of bloom: Amber yellow
Scent: Strong and spicy
Description of foliage: Dark green, somewhat red-tinted; glossy
Height and spread: 2½ x 4ft (75cm x 1.2m)
This is an excellent rose but it can be variable. Sometimes its flowers are more pink, and at other times they are more yellow. It seems to depend on the climate – a warm season appears to fade the flowers. There are usually 3–7 flowers in each cluster, and frequently more than this. It repeat-flowers reasonably well and is disease-resistant.

NAME: 'ANNE HARKNESS'

Origin: Harkness, UK (1979)
Parentage: 'Bobby Dazzler' x (['Manx Queen' x 'Prima Ballerina'] x ['Chanelle' x 'Harry Wheatcroft'])
USDA zone: 6
Description of bloom: Rich apricot yellow

ABOVE 'Anne Harkness'

Scent: Light and fruity
Description of foliage: Mid-green; matt and carried in quantity
Height and spread: 5 x 3ft (1.5m x 90cm)
This rose has beautiful, rich-apricot flowers. These appear when most other floribundas are resting before the first and second flushes, making this a valuable addition to the garden. Blooms come in clusters of 6–20, well-spaced on the stems.

NAME: 'ARTHUR BELL' AGM

Origin: McGredy, Northern Ireland (1965)
Parentage: 'Cläre Grammerstorf' x 'Harry Wheatcroft'
USDA zone: 5
Description of bloom: Yellow, fading to very pale yellow
Scent: Strong, rich and fruity
Description of foliage: Bright green; glossy and carried in quantity
Height and spread: 3 x 2½ft (90 x 75cm)
The main disadvantage of this rose – the fading of the flowers – is actually seen as an advantage by some gardeners: they open into a deep yellow, but quickly change to primrose, lemon and then cream. The stems are prickly, and the plant, in general, stands up well to rain.

ABOVE 'Arthur Bell' AGM

NAME: 'CHAMPAGNE COCKTAIL' AGM

Origin: Horner, UK (1983)
Parentage: 'Old Master' x 'Southampton'
USDA zone: 6
Description of bloom: Yellow, heavily suffused with pink
Scent: Delicate and sweet
Description of foliage: Dark green, semi-glossy
Height and spread: 3 x 2½ft (90 x 75cm)

In the early 1980s I was editor of a national UK gardening magazine and, with the late Colin Horner – an amateur rose breeder, living in the English county of Essex – agreed to run a competition with its readers to choose a name for his latest rose variety. We were inundated with suggestions, and Colin chose 'Champagne Cocktail', so I can say with some pride that I had a part in naming this award-winning rose! It was hailed as the first yellow 'hand-painted' rose (a term given to roses that have silvery petals with a strong colour feathered and blotched over the surface, leaving a white eye at the base) most of which are shades of rose-pink.

The colouring of this rose is fabulous: rich yellow, heavily suffused with pink, and a deeper pink on the reverse of the petals. Flowers are produced in clusters of 4–11.

NAME: 'EDITH HOLDEN'

Origin: Warner, UK (1988)
Parentage: 'Belinda' x ('Elizabeth of Glamis' x ['Galway Bay' x 'Sutters Gold'])
USDA zone: 6
Description of bloom: Dark, burnt orange
Scent: Light and fruity
Description of foliage: Medium to dark green, bronzy at first; glossy
Height and spread: 6½ft x 3ft (2m x 90cm)

The dark, burnt-orange, blooms of 'Edith Holden' fade to a dusky pink as they age. There is a bright yellow patch at the base of each petal and the yellow stamens in the centre stand out well against the petal colour. Blooms come in long-stemmed clusters of 5–11. It is a tall grower and, if left to its own devices, will throw out stems 10ft (3m) long.

ABOVE 'Edith Holden'

NAME: 'EYEPAINT'

Origin: McGredy, New Zealand (1975)
Parentage: seedling x 'Picasso'
USDA zone: 5
Description of bloom: Bright scarlet, with a white centre (or eye), and golden stamens
Scent: Delicate
Description of foliage: Dark green; abundant
Height and spread: 3 x 2½ft (90 x 75cm)
There are few roses that, when in full bloom, are as startlingly bright as this one. Blooms come in such profusion that they will cover the plant, which can get big. In warm weather, if left to its own devices, stems can extend to 6ft (2m) or more. Vigorous and disease-free, it is difficult to see how this variety could be bettered.

NAME: 'FESTIVAL FANFARE'

Origin: Ogilvie, UK (1982)
Parentage: sport of 'Fred Loads'
USDA zone: 5
Description of bloom: Pink blend; striped
Scent: Medium strength
Description of foliage: Dark green; matt
Height and spread: 6½ x 4ft (2 x 1.2m)
A very free-flowering sport of the old floribunda variety 'Fred Loads', this is a most attractive bi-coloured variety, boasting shades of deep salmon pink stripes with pale blush pink. It can be grown as a large shrub, or you can let it scramble into being a low climber. Blooms come in flushes throughout the season, and it doesn't mind whether the summer is hot, cold, wet or dry.

ABOVE **'Eyepaint'**

ABOVE **'Festival Fanfare'**

ABOVE 'Glenfiddich'

ABOVE 'Hot Chocolate'

NAME: 'GLENFIDDICH'

Origin: Cocker, UK (1976)
Parentage: 'Arthur Bell' x ('Sabine' x 'Circus')
USDA zone: 6
Description of bloom: Rich amber-yellow
Scent: Light and sweet
Description of foliage: Dark green; glossy
Height and spread: 3 x 3ft (90 x 90cm)
Possibly because of its very clean lines and simple structure, this rose is ideally suited to modern-style gardens and, if you could have a 'minimalist' floribunda rose, then this would be it. Bred in Aberdeen, a cold part of Scotland, it is a hardy plant with a rich, lush 'whisky' colour – hence its name (after a brand of whisky).

NAME: 'HOT CHOCOLATE'

Origin: Simpson, New Zealand (1986)
Parentage: 'Princess' x ('Tana' x 'Mary Summer')
USDA zone: 6

Description of bloom: Orange-brown, with occasional pale markings
Scent: Delicate, and reminiscent of apples (not hot chocolate!)
Description of foliage: Deep green; large
Height and spread: 3 x 2½ft (90 x 75cm)

This variety is extremely popular in Australia and New Zealand but seems to be slow to catch on in other parts of the world. It is a very unusual rose, with brownish flowers and white markings on some of the petals. Individually, the blooms are not very attractive, yet from a distance – when seen en masse – they are intriguing and quite different.

NAME: 'ICEBERG'
(SYN. 'SCHNEEWITTCHEN') AGM

Origin: Kordes, Germany (1958)
Parentage: 'Robin Hood' x 'Virgo'
USDA zone: 6
Description of bloom: Pure white, flushed pink in hot weather
Scent: Sweet, sometimes hardly discernible
Description of foliage: Bright green; glossy and produced in quantity
Height and spread: 4 x 2ft (1.2m x 60cm)

Some people have said that this is the best white floribunda rose. Others say it is the best floribunda of any colour. And still more reckon it is the most reliable of any white rose ever grown. Accolades indeed, but whichever camp you subscribe to, it cannot be denied that this is one fine rose. Floribunda roses are usually the progeny of a cross between a hybrid tea and a polyantha rose. 'Iceberg', however, is the result of breeding between a hybrid tea ('Virgo') and a hybrid musk rose ('Robin Hood'). It is this unusual pairing that may have resulted in the superior qualities of 'Iceberg'. It holds its colour, and its petals and flowers, well into autumn. There are fewer whites that are whiter, and it is pleasingly fragrant.

NAME: 'KORRESIA' (SYN. 'FRIESIA')

Origin: Kordes, Germany (1977)
Parentage: 'Friedrich Wörlein' x 'Spanish Sun'
USDA zone: 5
Description of bloom: Bright golden yellow
Scent: Strong and sweet
Description of foliage: Light green; glossy
Height and spread: 2½ x 2½ft (75 x 75cm)

I think that this is one of the best roses ever. Yellow is a fairly common colour amongst floribundas, but 'Korresia' is certainly in the top two or three of them. It is not, perhaps, as rich in colour as, say, 'Allgold', but it does have a better shape. More than most other roses I've grown, this variety seems to respond well to mulching. A good layer of well-rotted organic matter placed around the base of the plant – but not touching it – in spring means that the plant will be healthier, and probably, therefore, more intense in colour. 'Korresia' forms a small, upright bush and produces medium-sized double flowers of almost hybrid tea shape, but in small clusters. I love it.

ABOVE '**Iceberg**' AGM

ABOVE 'Lilli Marlene'

NAME: 'LILLI MARLENE'

Origin: Kordes, Germany (1959)
Parentage: ('Crimson Glow' x 'Rudolph Timm') x 'Ama'
USDA zone: 5
Description of bloom: Bright scarlet-crimson
Scent: Strong and sweet
Description of foliage: Dark green, bronze-tinted; glossy
Height and spread: 2½ x 2½ft (75 x 75cm)

A popular bedding rose, from the moment it was introduced. The bush has masses of foliage, and the flowers are abundant, too. Blackish buds open into velvety dark-red blooms which shrug off the effects of rain or hot sun. It has a good reputation for reliability and hardiness. Individually the blooms are not exceptional, but the overall effect of a mass of them from a distance is breathtaking.

NAME: 'MARGARET MERRILL' AGM

Origin: Harkness, UK (1977)
Parentage: ('Rudolph Timm' x 'Dedication') x 'Pascali'
USDA zone: 6
Description of bloom: White or pale blush pink
Scent: Very strong and sweet
Description of foliage: Dark green, leathery
Height and spread: 5 x 3ft (1.5m x 90cm)

Here is a white floribunda to compete with 'Iceberg'. In the battle of the whites, both varieties have their strong points: 'Iceberg' is perhaps whiter, whereas 'Margaret Merrill' is leaning more towards 'ivory' or 'pearl'. But the form and fragrance of the individual flowers of 'Margaret Merrill', and the general health and resistance this variety has to disease, beat 'Iceberg' hands down. There are few rose varieties that have won as many awards.

NAME: 'MASQUERADE'

Origin: Boerner, US (1949)
Parentage: 'Goldilocks' x 'Holiday'
USDA zone: 5
Description of bloom: Yellow, turning through salmon pink to red
Scent: Delicate and musky
Description of foliage: Dark green; small in size and matt
Height and spread: 3 x 3ft (90 x 90cm)

This was the first rose to be grown by the general public that produced individual flowers of different colours: when the buds open, the semi-double flower is bright yellow, then as it ages it turns into a rose-pink, followed by a bright crimson before the petals drop. From early summer until early autumn all the colours are present at the same time. This, depending on your view, is breathtakingly beautiful and incredibly intriguing, or it is a 'freak of nature' and has no place in an ornamental garden. It responds particularly well to deadheading.

NAME: 'MOUNTBATTEN' AGM

Origin: Harkness, UK (1982)
Parentage: 'Peer Gynt' (['Anne Cocker' x 'Arthur Bell'] x 'Southampton')
USDA zone: 6
Description of bloom: Yellow
Scent: Strong, sweet and fruity
Description of foliage: Dark green; matt and produced in quantity
Height and spread: 5 x 3ft (1.5m x 90cm)

Named after Earl Mountbatten of Burma, this was the 'Rose of the Year' for 1982, the year of its launch. An outstanding variety, it produces delightfully conspicuous trusses of mimosa-yellow flowers. Growing somewhat taller than average and stands as a slim, commanding bush. Highly recommended for bedding and useful for hedging, with a pleasant fragrance and a high resistance to disease.

BELOW 'Mountbatten' AGM

ABOVE 'Penelope' AGM

NAME: 'PENELOPE' AGM

Origin: Pemberton, UK (1924)
Parentage: 'Trier' x 'Ophelia'
USDA zone: 7
Description of bloom: Pale cream and blush-pink, fading to white
Scent: Sweet and musky

Description of foliage: Dark green; semi-glossy and large
Height and spread: 6½ x 6½ft (2 x 2m)
Although technically a floribunda, this variety is often listed in catalogues as a hybrid musk variety. This is because it is a hybrid, and its flowers have a very musky fragrance. Its charm comes from its prolific blooming, rather than the status of individual flowers. This is one of the best roses for massed colour during the quieter autumn months.

NAME: 'PURPLE TIGER'

Origin: Jackson & Perkins, US (1991)
Parentage: 'Intrigue' x 'Pinstripe'
USDA zone: 6
Description of bloom: Purple and ivory stripes
Scent: Light and sweet
Description of foliage: Mid-green; glossy
Height and spread: 3 x 2½ft (90 x 75cm)
I love this rose, for its unusual colouring and patterning. It is aptly named, and its vivid striped flowers make a real talking point.

ABOVE 'Purple Tiger'

'Purple Tiger' is the sort of rose you will either love, or hate. The full blooms are carried on fairly short stems and set off by mid-green foliage. It also has a very useful potential for flower-arranging.

NAME: 'QUEEN ELIZABETH'

Origin: Lammerts, US (1954)
Parentage: 'Charlotte Armstrong' x 'Floradora'
USDA zone: 6
Description of bloom: Pale pink with darker pink reverse
Scent: Medium and sweet
Description of foliage: Dark green; large in size and leathery
Height and spread: 8 x 3¼ft (2.5 x 1m)
This is one of the best-loved roses of all time. Pure, pale-pink flowers, beautifully shaped, are carried on strong stems from early summer to late autumn. Although a floribunda, its habit is vigorous and upright, making it a good hedging rose or even a specimen bush. It is best pruned hard each year, which results in a denser shrub,

and helps to keep its vigour under control. It is excellent for growing at the back of a border, and is also good as a cut flower. May also be sold under the similar name of 'The Queen Elizabeth Rose'.

NAME: 'RHAPSODY IN BLUE'

Origin: Warner, UK (2003)
Parentage: Not disclosed
USDA zone: 6
Description of bloom: Dark purple, fading to lilac-grey
Scent: Strongly fragrant
Description of foliage: Mid-green and glossy
Height and spread: 3 x 3ft (90 x 90cm)
This was named 'Rose of the Year' in 2003 and is arguably the most exciting new release for decades. Its unique colour is captivating and the closest yet to blue. The flowers, which are large, semi-double and open fully, are carried in big clusters on a medium-growing plant with shrubby growth. It is something different for mixed borders and adds a new dimension to theme plantings.

ABOVE 'Rhapsody in Blue'

ABOVE **'Ripples'**

NAME: **'RIPPLES'**

Origin: LeGrice, UK (1971)
Parentage: ('Tantau's Surprise' x 'Marjorie LeGrice') x (seedling x 'Africa Star')
USDA zone: 6
Description of bloom: Lilac-lavender
Scent: Medium strength
Description of foliage: Mid-green, matt
Height and spread: 20 x 20in (50 x 50cm)
The stunning bluish flowers of this rose are produced abundantly throughout the growing season. It is a dwarf floribunda, which is perfect for the front of a border, or in a container, where its stunning flowers can be seen at close quarters.

NAME: **'SCENTIMENTAL'**

Origin: Carruth, US (1996)
Parentage: 'Playboy' x 'Peppermint Twist'
USDA zone: 6
Description of bloom: Cherry-crimson and blush-pink or white striped
Scent: Strong and sweet
Description of foliage: Blue-green; matt
Height and spread: 4 x 3ft (1.2m x 90cm)
'Scentimental' is one of the best of the modern, striped roses. Like a hybrid tea, it has large flowers, often 6in (15cm) across. The flowers come in quite small clusters but, because of the size and colour of the individuals, there is quite an impact when clustered together.

ABOVE 'Scentimental'

This variety has a powerful scent, too, hence its name. But it is the thick, striped petals of the flowers which separate this rose from all others: some blooms are white with a few stripes of dark pink, whilst others are cherry-crimson with a few blush-pink stripes – and yet others are different combinations of the same. It repeat-flowers well, but the best blooms appear in cool summers.

ABOVE 'Sexy Rexy' AGM

NAME: 'SEXY REXY' AGM

Origin: McGredy, New Zealand (1984)
Parentage: 'Seaspray' x 'Traumerei'
USDA zone: 6
Description of bloom: Light rose-pink
Scent: Delicate
Description of foliage: Dark green; glossy and carried in quantity
Height and spread: 2½ x 2ft (75 x 60cm)

In spite of – or maybe because of – its memorable name, this rose has sold incredibly well. Its superior rose-pink blooms open out flat, each petal becoming paler towards the edges, and with a slightly darker reverse. It is not unusual to have clusters of 15 flowers, which makes for a breathtaking head of colour. As the blooms come a little later in the season than those of other floribundas, and it is slow to produce a second flush, this variety is useful as it effectively prolongs the flowering season of floribundas.

ABOVE 'Southampton' AGM

NAME: 'SOUTHAMPTON' AGM

Origin: Harkness, UK (1971)
Parentage: ('Anne Elizabeth' x 'Allgold') x 'Yellow Cushion'
USDA zone: 6
Description of bloom: Apricot, flushed with orange and pale scarlet
Scent: Medium and sweet
Description of foliage: Dark green; glossy
Height and spread: 5 x 3ft (1.5cm x 90cm)

Named after the city of Southampton, on England's south coast, for many years this rose was considered the best floribunda of all. The apricot, orange and salmon blooms pale slightly and become pinker as they age but, at every stage in the flower's life, it is handsome. The semi-double flowers stand up well to the elements, and are almost large enough to be thought of as a hybrid tea variety. The clusters can be of any number between 3–11.

ABOVE 'Stargazer'

NAME: 'STARGAZER'

Origin: Harkness, UK (1977)
Parentage: 'Marlena' x 'Kim'
USDA zone: 6
Description of bloom: Yellow-orange blend
Scent: Light
Description of foliage: Mid-green, medium-sized and matt
Height and spread: 5 x 3ft (1.5m x 90cm)
A very good rose, which is best when planted in a group – preferably a large group. Set individual plants 3ft (90cm) apart and you will not be disappointed with the results.

NAME: 'SUNNY ABUNDANCE'

Origin: Harkness, UK (2001)
Parentage: Not disclosed
USDA zone: 6
Description of bloom: Yellow and pink blend
Scent: Medium strength; fruity
Description of foliage: Dark green; glossy and large in size
Height and spread: 3 x 2ft (90 x 60cm)
This rose is extremely resistant to diseases and

flowers almost perpetually throughout the growing season. It is one of a number of roses with the 'Abundance' name from Harkness, all known for their reliability and vigour. They are also recommended for combination plantings, so are ideal for crowded cottage-style gardens and amongst herbaceous perennials.

ABOVE 'Sunny Abundance'

133

ABOVE 'Tawny Tiger'

NAME: **'TAWNY TIGER'**

Origin: Fryer, UK (2003)
Parentage: Not disclosed
USDA zone: 6
Description of bloom: Russet-brown, striped with terracotta
Scent: Little
Description of foliage: Mid-green; matt
Height and spread: 2½ x 2½ft (75 x 75cm)
This is an extraordinary floribunda, with brown and terracotta stripes – a definite colour breakthrough. Semi-double flowers of rich dark orange are amazingly striped, and rippled with terracotta and brown which attractively combine to great dramatic effect. 'Tawny Tiger' is bushy and loaded with blooms, and is certain to provide a very interesting discussion point, especially when it is planted at the front of a mixed border.

NAME: **'TRUMPETER'** AGM

Origin: McGredy, New Zealand (1977)
Parentage: seedling of 'Satchmo'
USDA zone: 6
Description of bloom: Dark orange-scarlet
Scent: Delicate
Description of foliage: Dark green, with a purplish tinge at first; glossy
Height and spread: 2ft x 18in (60 x 45cm)
This rose has shapely, well-filled flowers of dark orange-scarlet, abundant all summer long, on a neat, bushy, low-growing plant. 'Trumpeter' is superb for bedding, mass planting and specimen planting. What it lacks in stature, it makes up for in usefulness around the garden.

ABOVE **'Trumpeter'** AGM

NAME: **'VALENTINE HEART'** AGM

Origin: Dickson, Northern Ireland (1989)
Parentage: 'Shona' x 'Pot o' Gold'
USDA zone: 6
Description of bloom: Blush pink
Scent: Strong and sweet
Description of foliage: Dark green; glossy and carried in quantity
Height and spread: 4 x 2½ft (1.2m x 75cm)
'Valentine Heart' is an enchanting soft pink with a powerful fragrance and it is definitely one for the romantics amongst us. Growth is strong and healthy, producing a wealth of flowers that, rather pleasingly, seem to be unaffected by weather.

ABOVE 'Valentine Heart' AGM

OTHER FLORIBUNDA ROSES WORTHY OF NOTE:

As with the hybrid teas, there are masses of other floribunda roses that really do deserve to have a place in our rose gardens, but we do not have the space here to describe them. They include:

'Allgold': Buttercup yellow.
'Anisley Dickson' AGM: Salmon-pink, to coral.
'Anna Livia' AGM: Salmon-pink.

'Atlantic Star': Blend of apricot and peach.
'City of Belfast': Velvety orange-scarlet.
'City of Leeds': Rich salmon pink.
'Cliff Richard': Medium pink.
'Dearest': Salmon to rose pink.
'English Miss' AGM: Silver-pink, edged with deeper pink.
'Elizabeth of Glamis': Bright salmon pink, fading to rose pink.
'Evelyn Fison': Dark scarlet-red, non-fading.

ABOVE 'Anna Livia' AGM

ABOVE 'Atlantic Star'

ABOVE 'Cliff Richard'

ABOVE 'Fern's Rose'

'Eyecatcher': Blend of pinks.

'Fern's Rose': Cream-yellow.

'Fragrant Delight' AGM: Pale orange-pink.

'Free Spirit': Salmon pink.

'Glad Tidings': Deep crimson.

'Golden Wedding': Deep, golden yellow.

'Many Happy Returns' AGM: Blush pink.

'Matangi' AGM: Vermillion with a white eye.

'Melody Maker': Blend of orange-red.

'Piccolo': Coral-red.

'Pink Parfait': Pink with cream to the base of the bloom.

'Regensberg': White bud flushed pink opening to reveal deeper pink and white.

'Remembrance' AGM: Deep bright scarlet.

'Singing in the Rain' (syn. 'Spek's Centennial'): Smoky pink to apricot.

'Tickled Pink': Soft rose-pink.

'Varenna Allen': Pale apricot-orange.

ABOVE **'Fragrant Delight' AGM**

ABOVE **'Free Spirit'**

ABOVE **'Singing in the Rain'**

ABOVE **'Tickled Pink'**

SHRUB AND HEDGING ROSES

There are hundreds of species and varieties of 'shrub rose' which are divided into many different races, styles and groups. They probably account for more than three quarters of the total number of roses. A book of this size can merely skim the surface of the wide range available, but I hope that it will also inspire you to delve more into the subject, by consulting other publications that specialize in them.

OLD-FASHIONED ROSES

Most shrub roses come into this category. In general terms they are the roses that were grown in the larger gardens of the nineteenth and early twentieth centuries, in the gardening years before hybrid teas and floribundas. These old-fashioned roses can be further divided into the following styles.

Alba: These are easily recognized by their soft, drooping grey-green foliage. They are vigorous plants that usually require rigorous pruning to keep them in check. They generally repel pests and diseases. Flowers appear in a single flush in mid-summer, and they are pink or white, and highly scented. These are the best roses for growing in a shady part of the garden.

Bourbon: In the early 1800s a hybrid occurred between an autumn-flowering damask rose and a China rose – and the bourbon group was born. The fragrant, rounded flowers, comprising many large petals, bloom in autumn as well as early summer and they quickly became sought after for Victorian gardens. You can still buy them today, but they have largely been superceded by the hybrid perpetuals (see below), so you will have to go to specialist nurseries to find them.

Centifolia: This is sometimes called the cabbage rose because of its double, globular flowers. These are not perfect garden plants, in that the stems are lax and need supporting if they are to be shown off to their best. They are not as sturdy, nor as robust as alba or rugosa roses, but they do have lovely colours and, invariably, a powerfully strong fragrance.

ABOVE 'Madame Isaac Pereire' AGM – a Bourbon rose.

ABOVE 'Petite de Hollande' – a centifolia rose.

ABOVE 'Complicata' AGM – a gallica rose.

China: The China roses have been very important in the development of modern hybrid bush and shrub varieties. They generally have a slender, open habit and bear large clusters of small flowers throughout summer. Unfortunately they are not always hardy, and will suffer in cold or exposed positions.

Damask: The fragrance is incredibly powerful and is the first thing one thinks of when talking about damask roses (which are forms of *Rosa damascena*). The habit of these plants is not always popular, however. The arching stems are weak, usually causing the flowers to droop, and the foliage is considered to be dull by most rosarians. Blooms come in a single mid-summer flush. The historical roses of the British Royal Houses of York and Lancaster are damasks.

Gallica: These are ideal for anyone interested in old shrub roses, but who only has room for a few. They do not generally grow bigger than 4ft (1.2m) in height. Usually flowering in the early summer, they offer a fairly limited range of colours. They are derived from the single, pink-flowered *Rosa gallica*, and many of them existed before the seventeenth century. The better forms, however, have been bred in the last 150 years.

Hybrid musk: At the beginning of the twentieth century an Englishman, the Rev. Joseph Pemberton, introduced and named this group of roses. They are scented like the old musk rose, but are not particularly closely linked to it. They flower in early summer, and produce a particularly good second flush in early autumn.

Hybrid perpetual: Towards the end of Queen Victoria's reign, this type of rose became the most popular throughout her Empire. A few of the thousands of varieties are still available, but the modern hybrids have taken over in the popularity stakes.

ABOVE 'Ferdinand Pichard' AGM – a hybrid perpetual.

ABOVE *'Blanc Double de Coubert' AGM – a rugosa hybrid.*

In fact, hybrid perpetuals are not 'perpetual' – they actually have two distinct flower flushes. The flowers are cup-shaped, and the plants are quite vigorous for small gardens.

Moss: Around 1700, an unknown centifolia rose produced a sport, which bore masses of distinctive sticky 'hairs' in brown or green all over the upper parts of the flower stalks, and the green parts of the flower bases (the 'sepals'). This became the first moss rose, and many have been developed since. The highly fragrant blooms appear just once in summer.

Polyantha: A group of very hardy, low-growing shrub roses, rarely reaching taller than 3ft (90cm). These plants produce large clusters of small roses, more or less continuously throughout summer and well into autumn. These were the forerunners of the floribundas, and have been more or less superceded by them.

Rugosa: Both the original *Rosa rugosa*, and its many modern hybrids are hardy, tolerant roses; they will grow in poor soils and exposed places where most other types of rose would perish. These plants are dense, thorny and tall, and are therefore considered to be the best types of rose to grow for hedging.

MODERN SHRUB ROSES

This is a widely diverse group of roses with little in common, apart from the fact that they have been available since the 1970s. Most, but not all, are repeat-flowering. Examples are the many dozens of excellent varieties to come from the David Austin nursery in England, where a number of them have been grouped together and classed as 'English' roses.

SPECIES ROSES

All wild roses are included in this group, together with their close relatives. They can be referred to by their Latin names, but many also are known by their common names. Examples are *Rosa laevigata* and *R. canina*, also known respectively as the wild rose and dog rose. Most species roses tend to bloom only once a year, and this is usually before the majority of hybrid teas and floribundas get into full swing. The origin of most species roses is lost in history, or was never known.

HEDGING ROSES

Rugosa roses are the best of all roses for making boundary hedges. The prickly stems are child-, intruder- and animal-proof, many forms produce attractive hips in late autumn and winter, and the handsome foliage is mildew-free. The rugosa varieties 'Scabrosa' AGM and 'Roseraie de l'Hay' AGM take pride of place for this.

The hybrid musks are another popular group for hedging. One variety ('Penelope' – listed on page128, under 'Floribundas', because of its cluster-flowering habit) is superior.

Another floribunda, 'Queen Elizabeth' has become a favourite hedging rose, but it can be disappointing if you do not know what its drawbacks are. The secret is to prune the stems to different heights, so that the flowers and foliage are carried at varying heights, instead of just at the top, which makes for denser cover. Here, some of the best shrub roses are shown.

PICTORIAL SELECTION OF SHRUB AND HEDGING ROSES

The list here is by no means complete, but includes some of the leading examples in the huge range of several hundred species and varieties. All of the roses pictured are available commercially, although you may need to approach specialist rose nurseries to find some of them.

'CHARLES RENNIE MACKINTOSH'
Modern shrub rose (Austin, UK 1998)

ROSA X ALBA 'ALBA SEMIPLENA' AGM
Species rose (first cultivated c.1500)

'COUNTESS OF WESSEX'
Modern shrub rose (Beales, UK 2004)

'ALNWICK CASTLE'
Modern shrub rose (Austin, UK 2001)

ROSA CANINA
Species rose (the 'dog rose'; originated throughout Europe and south-west Asia)

ROSA DAVIDII
Species rose (wild rose; originated in China)

'DUCHESSE D'ANGOULÊME'
Gallica (Vibert, France 1821)

'FETZER SYRAH ROSE'
Modern shrub rose (Harkness, UK 2006)

'EGLANTYNE' AGM
Modern shrub rose (Austin, UK 1994)

'FIMBRIATA'
Rugosa hybrid (Morlet, France 1891)

'ERFURT'
Shrub rose (Kordes, Germany 1931)

'FRITZ NOBIS' AGM
Shrub rose (Kordes, Germany 1940)

'FRÜHLINGSGOLD' AGM
Shrub rose (Kordes, Germany (1937)

'GERTRUDE JEKYLL' AGM
Modern shrub rose (Austin, UK 1986)

'GOLDEN WINGS' AGM
Shrub rose (Shepherd, US 1958)

'GRAHAM THOMAS' AGM
Modern shrub rose (Austin, UK 1983)

'HEBE'S LIP' (SYN. 'RUBROTINCTA')
Damask rose (Lee, UK 1846)

'HORATIO NELSON'
Modern shrub rose (Beales, UK 1997)

'JACQUELINE DU PRÉ' AGM
Modern shrub rose (Harkness, UK 1988)

143

'JOHN HOPPER'
Hybrid perpetual (Ward, UK 1862)

'LILIAN AUSTIN'
Shrub rose (Austin, UK 1973)

'MARJORIE FAIR' AGM
Polyantha rose (Harkness, UK 1978)

'MARY MAGDALENE'
Modern shrub rose (Austin, UK 1999)

'MARY ROSE' AGM
Modern shrub rose (Austin, UK 1983)

'MOLINEUX' AGM
Modern shrub rose (Austin, UK 1994)

'MRS JOHN LAING'
Hybrid perpetual (Bennett, UK 1887)

'NYVELDT'S WHITE'
Rugosa hybrid
(Nyveldt, The Netherlands 1955)

'REDOUTÉ'
Modern shrub rose (Austin, UK 1992)

'OFFICINALIS'
Gallica rose; cultivated variety dating from
c. 1400

ROSA X RICHARDII
Natural hybrid between two species roses
(probably between *R. gallica* and *R. arvensis*)

'RAYMOND CARVER'
Modern shrub rose (Horner, UK 1999)

'SCARLET FIRE' (SYN. 'SCHARLACHGLUT') AGM
Shrub rose (Kordes, Germany 1952)

'SHROPSHIRE LASS'
Modern shrub rose (Austin, UK 1968)

'THE COUNTRYMAN'
Modern shrub rose (Austin, UK 1987)

'THE HERBALIST'
Modern shrub rose (Austin, UK 1991)

'TRADESCANT'
Modern shrub rose (Austin, UK 1994)

'VERSICOLOR' AGM
Gallica rose; cultivated variety (c. 1550)

'WILLIAM LOBB' AGM
Moss rose (Laffay, France 1855)

'WINCHESTER CATHEDRAL'
Modern shrub rose (Austin, UK 1992)

OTHER SHRUBS AND HEDGING ROSES

There are, literally, hundreds of shrub roses, many of which are interesting botanically but which do not make particularly good garden plants. Here are a few that deserve mention, but for which we do not have the space to describe fully.

'Ballerina' AGM: Rose-pink with white centres.
Rosa biebersteinii: Cream-white, single.
'Boule de Neige': Slightly pink in bud opening to pure white.
'Buff Beauty' AGM: Yellow-peach.
'Céleste' AGM: Pink with yellow stamens.
Rosa eglanteria (syn. *R. rubiginosa*): Pink, single.
'Fantin-Latour' AGM: Shell pink.
'Felicia' AGM: Pink.
'Frau Dagmar Hastrup' AGM: Pale silver-pink, single.
Rosa gallica 'Cardinal de Richelieu' AGM: Rich burgundy-purple.
Rosa gallica 'Charles de Mills' AGM: Rich crimson-purple.
'Königin von Dänemark' AGM: Pink, double.
'La Reine Victoria': Lilac-pink.
'Mme Alfred Carrière' AGM: White, sometimes with a slight hint of pink.

ABOVE 'Fantin-Latour' AGM

'Mortimer Sackler': Pure, soft rose-pink.
Rosa moyesii: Pink to red, single.
Rosa moyesii 'Geranium' AGM: Deep pink to red, single, with excellent autumn hips.
Rosa x odorata 'Mutabilis' AGM: Yellow, through apricot to pink and red.
Rosa pimpinellifolia: Cream-white, single.
'Radio Times': Soft, salmon-pink.
'Roseraie de l'Hay' AGM: Dark red-purple.
'Sarah van Fleet': Pink, gold stamens.
'Scabrosa' AGM: Deep rose-pink with cream-yellow stamens.
'Souvenir de la Malmaison': Salmon-pink, from coppery buds.
Rosa virginiana AGM: Rich pink with gold stamens.

ABOVE 'Ballerina' AGM

ABOVE 'Radio Times'

CLIMBING AND RAMBLER ROSES

Ramblers are distinct from climbing roses in that they ramble anywhere and everywhere, unless controlled. They often have very long, pliable shoots, flower almost exclusively in the early summer, and generally produce a huge number of quite small flowers.

Climbing roses, on the other hand, climb in a measured way, and their blooms are usually fewer but individually larger.

Climbing roses, the more numerous of the two types, are split into several distinct sub-divisions:

1 Older climbers, such as 'Zépherine Drouhin' and 'Mme Alfred Carrière' AGM that date back to the mid-nineteenth century.

2 Modern climbers, such as 'Golden Showers' and 'Aloha' AGM, which were bred or developed in recent years.

3 Those that started life as bush hybrid teas or floribundas, but have been sported, or otherwise bred, into a climbing form – more often the case with hybrid teas such as 'Climbing Peace', and 'Climbing Ena Harkness' than with floribundas.

NAME: 'ALBÉRIC BARBIER' AGM

Origin: Barbier, France (1900)
Parentage: *Rosa wichurana* x 'Shirley Hibberd'
USDA zone: 7

Description of bloom: Cream-white, opening from yellow buds
Scent: Delicate and sweet
Description of foliage: Dark green; glossy and semi-evergreen
Height and spread: 15 x 12ft (5 x 4m)
This rambler is not very hardy, so it performs best in warmer climates. Individually the flowers are variable, from semi-double with golden stamens, to messy double petals seemingly growing in all directions. Standing back, however, the overall effect of the plant can be stunning. It looks good growing through a small tree, or along a fence.

NAME: 'ALOHA' AGM

Origin: Boerner, US (1949)
Parentage: 'Mércèdes Gallart' x 'New Dawn'
USDA zone: 5
Description of bloom: Rose-pink with coppery-pink tones
Scent: Strong and fruity
Description of foliage: Dark green, bronze-tinted; leathery, very glossy and abundant
Height and spread: 10 x 6½ft (3 x 2m)
This modern climber is widely thought to be one of the best. Each bloom is packed full of petals,

ABOVE 'Altissimo'

ABOVE 'Breath of Life'

and it opens out into a wide, flat, reflexed flower. All the petals have paler edges and, although the overall colouring is rose-pink, there are distinctive shades of red, crimson, salmon-pink and even terracotta. It is a slow grower, but is prone to rust and mildew in some seasons.

NAME 'ALTISSIMO'

Origin: Delbard-Chabert, France (1966)
Parentage: seedling of 'Ténor'
USDA zone: 6
Description of bloom: Unfading bright red, revealing golden stamens; single
Scent: Little
Description of foliage: Dark green, large in size and matt
Height and spread: 10 x 6½ft (3 x 2m)
This is a modern climber with intense red flowers. The flowers do not fade, either in bright sunlight or through age, although their colouring is stronger in cooler weather. Blooms come in small clusters on long stems, almost constantly from early summer to mid-autumn.

NAME: 'BREATH OF LIFE'

Origin: Harkness, UK (1980)
Parentage: 'Red Dandy' x 'Alexander'
USDA zone: 6
Description of bloom: Apricot-pink aging to clear pink
Scent: Medium strength; sweet and musky
Description of foliage: Mid-green; semi-glossy
Height and spread: 6½ x 4ft (2m x 1.2m)
Although this is technically a shrub rose, it is very upright in habit and is therefore often sold as a climber. If growing against a wall it can usually stretch way beyond the height and spread mentioned. Blackspot may be a problem, however, especially towards the end of the growing season.

149

ABOVE 'Compassion' AGM

ABOVE 'Dorothy Perkins'

NAME: 'COMPASSION' AGM

Origin: Harkness, UK (1972)
Parentage: 'White Cockade' x 'Prima Ballerina'
USDA zone: 6
Description of bloom: Rosy salmon-pink with apricot tints
Scent: Strong and sweet
Description of foliage: Dark green; large, glossy and plentiful
Height and spread: 10 x 6½ft (3 x 2m)

When the flowers of this modern climber open they are a beautiful mixture of salmon-pink with hints of apricot and even orange. As they age, however, they turn to a dirty white, and stay on the plant for a long time before dropping; as a consequence, at the peak of the season you have a plant with a mishmash of strong pinks and apricots and the dirty whites, which can spoil the whole effect. However, the leaves always appear healthy and the plant is not particularly susceptible to fungal diseases.

NAME: 'DOROTHY PERKINS'

Origin: Jackson & Perkins, US (1901)
Parentage: seedling of 'Turner's Crimson Rambler'
USDA zone: 5
Description of bloom: Rose-pink; carried in long, open clusters
Scent: Light
Description of foliage: Mid- to dark green; small, glossy and abundant
Height and spread: 13 x 6½ft (4 x 2m)

In the early 1900s this rambler rose – named after the daughter of a business contact of the breeders – caused a sensation, as its vivid pink colour and heady fragrance were far stronger than any other rambler of the time. Years later, a London drapery firm opened a shop and named it after the most popular rose of the day. That shop has grown into Dorothy Perkins, the popular chain of ladies' clothes shops throughout the UK. Because of the ease with which cuttings can be taken, gardeners would propagate it themselves and pass it on to neighbours, so that over time whole neighbourhoods were decorated with it. By the 1930s the rose was seen growing everywhere.

NAME: 'DREAMING SPIRES'

Origin: Mattock, UK (1973)
Parentage: seedling of 'Arthur Bell' x 'Allgold'
USDA zone: 6
Description of bloom: Bright yellow with a hint of orange
Scent: Medium strength and fruity
Description of foliage: Dark blue-green; carried in quantity
Height and spread: 10 x 8ft (3m x 2.5m)
This is one of the first roses to open in the year. Its lightly double flowers are a strong yellow, each petal being darker on the reverse at first, but fading as they age. In warm weather the flowers can fade to near-white. It repeat-flowers well, and can offer some particularly good, but far fewer, blooms in the autumn.

NAME: 'FÉLICITÉ ET PERPÉTUE' AGM

Origin: Jacques, France (1827)
Parentage: *Rosa sempervirens* x 'Old Blush'
USDA zone: 5
Description of bloom: Red buds opening to cream-white
Scent: Delicate; musky
Description of foliage: Dark green; small, pointed and semi-evergreen
Height and spread: 15 x 12ft (5m x 4m)
An old climbing rose with masses of small, densely packed rosette flowers. The main problem with this plant is that it does not shed its flowers until the very last moment, which means you have lots of lovely white flowers at the same time as lots of faded brown flowers, which can spoil the whole appearance. It is a thick and vigorous grower, however, which more than makes up for this shortcoming.

ABOVE **'Dreaming Spires'**

ABOVE **'Golden Showers' AGM**

NAME: 'GOLDEN SHOWERS' AGM

Origin: Lammerts, US (1956)
Parentage: 'Charlotte Armstrong' x 'Captain Thomas'
USDA zone: 7
Description of bloom: Deep gold-yellow fading to cream-yellow
Scent: Medium strength and sweet
Description of foliage: Dark green; glossy
Height and spread: 10 x 6½ft (3 x 2m) ▶

ABOVE '**Good as Gold**'

NAME: 'GOOD AS GOLD'

Origin: Warner, UK (1994)
Parentage: 'Anne Harkness' x 'Laura Ford'
USDA zone: 6
Description of bloom: Golden-yellow
Scent: Light and fruity
Description of foliage: Dark green; small, narrow and glossy
Height and spread: 8 x 6½ft (2.5 x 2m)
This has been described both as a 'climbing miniature' and a 'patio climber'. Whichever is your favourite term for it, the truth is that it is a very good and reliable rose. The blooms are not large but they are well-shaped, and of a clear golden yellow, with slightly darker tones on the petal reverse.

NAME: 'KIFTSGATE' AGM

Origin: Murrell, UK (1954)
Parentage: Wild rose, generally thought to be a form of *Rosa filipes* (China)
USDA zone: 6
Description of bloom: Creamy white
Scent: Strong and musky
Description of foliage: Fresh, mid-green; large and glossy
Height and spread: 33 x 13ft (10 x 4m)
The heritage of this rose is not 100 per cent certain, but it is believed to be a natural variety of *Rosa filipes*, a Chinese climber. It was first spotted as a seedling in the garden of Kiftsgate Court, a garden in the county of Gloucestershire, England. The original plant, which is still growing, is some 82ft (25m) in length, so be warned! Although it can be kept under control, it is not to be recommended for small gardens. The flowers are small, single and creamy white. They come in such profusion, often with more than 100 blooms in a cluster, that there are few roses to rival it. In the autumn, it is covered with small, bright orange hips.

'Golden Showers' is one of the best-known yellow climbers, never failing to give a good account of itself during the summer months. Flowers are loosely double, with a distinct ruffle to the petals, and red-brown stamens. The main flush of flower is in early summer, blooms thereafter come in ones and twos. It stands up well to rain.

OPPOSITE TOP *Rosa filipes* '**Kiftsgate**' AGM

NAME: 'MME GRÉGOIRE STAECHELIN' AGM

Origin: Dot, Spain (1927)
Parentage: 'Frau Karl Druschki' x 'Chateau de Clos Vougeot'
USDA zone: 6
Description of bloom: Clear pink, with hints of rich carmine
Scent: Strongly fragrant; sweet
Description of foliage: Dark green, matt
Height and spread: 20 x 12ft (6 x 4m)

A modern climber with masses of tightly packed deep-pink flowers, this is one of the best for scent and the blooms hang in such a way that you can see right in to their centres. The pink and carmine petals are paler at the edges. Introduced by Pedro Dot, Spain's greatest rose hybridist, whose work spanned more than 50 years.

NAME: 'NEW DAWN' (SYN. 'DR W. VAN FLEET') AGM

Origin: Van Fleet, US (1910)
Parentage: (*Rosa wichurana* x 'Safrano') x 'Souvenir du Président Carnot'
USDA zone: 5
Description of bloom: Very pale pink
Scent: Medium strength and sweet ▶

NAME: 'MME ALFRED CARRIÈRE' AGM

Origin: Schwartz, France (1879)
Parentage: Unknown
USDA zone: 7
Description of bloom: Milky white
Scent: Fresh and sweet
Description of foliage: Pale green; large and carried in quantity
Height and spread: 18 x 10ft (5.5 x 3m)

In climates such as the Mediterranean, and other warm maritime areas, this rose can flower all year round. In the cooler regions, however, it will be one of the first roses to flower, and last all summer and most of the autumn. Long, elegant pink buds open to white, and each individual bloom stays in colour for a long time. The plant does not have many thorns.

ABOVE 'New Dawn' AGM

Description of foliage: Rich green; semi-glossy and abundant

Height and spread: 16 x 6½ft (5 x 2m)

'New Dawn' is a fabulous rambler that flowers perpetually, from early summer until early winter. The blooms are large and pale pink, almost fading to white towards the edges of the petals. 'Weisse New Dawn' is a white-flowering sport of 'New Dawn'.

NAME: 'PAUL'S HIMALAYAN MUSK' AGM

Origin: Paul, UK (1916)

Parentage: *Rosa brunonii* x a Moschata hybrid

USDA zone: 6

Description of bloom: Blush pink to lilac pink

Scent: Light and musky

ABOVE 'Pink Perpêtue'

Description of foliage: Light green; long, pointed and drooping

Height and spread: 30 x 30ft (10 x 10m)

One of the most vigorous of ramblers, the small flowers come in clusters of up to 50, and have petals arranged in a pretty rosette. After a few days each flower fades to white. It is the most perfect rose for rambling through a large, old tree.

NAME: 'PINK PERPÊTUE'

Origin: Gregory, UK (1965)

Parentage: 'Danse du Feu' x 'New Dawn'

USDA zone: 5

Description of bloom: Clear pink; darker at base

Scent: Light

Description of foliage: Mid-green; glossy, leathery and plentiful

Height and spread: 10 x 8ft (3m x 2.5m)

This medium-size climber performs best in a cooler climate. The flowers are clear pink on the upper sides, and carmine on the reverse. They are not particularly tolerant of the weather, however: the colour can bleach in the sun, and become blotched in the rain. The stems are thorny, and the leaves can be susceptible to blackspot. But this is one of the finest pink climbers for autumn flowers.

NAME: 'RAMBLING RECTOR' AGM

Origin: Daisy Hill, Northern Ireland (c. 1900)

Parentage: Thought to be *Rosa multiflora* x *Rosa moschata*

USDA zone: 6

Description of bloom: Creamy-white with golden stamens

Scent: Sweet and fresh

Description of foliage: Light to mid-green; semi-glossy and plentiful

Height and spread: 10 x 6ft (3 x 2m)

This rambler has a mysterious history. It is thought to be a chance seedling, found in a garden in Northern Ireland, but nobody knows for sure.

It carries large, loose clusters of small semi-double flowers – perhaps up to 50 in number – which are followed by small orange hips in autumn.

NAME: 'SPIRIT OF FREEDOM'

Origin: Austin, UK (2002)
Parentage: Not disclosed
USDA zone: 6
Description of bloom: Soft pink
Scent: Medium strength, sweet
Description of foliage: Mid-green; semi-glossy
Height and spread: 8 x 8ft (2.5 x 2.5m)
This variety boasts large, pure, soft-pink blooms each containing more than 150 beautifully arranged petals. Apart from the beauty of its flowers, this rose is grown for its healthy nature, being immune to most of the common pests and diseases of roses.

NAME: 'ZÉPHERINE DROUHIN'

Origin: Bizot, France (1868)
Parentage: Not known
USDA zone: 5
Description of bloom: Deep carmine pink
Scent: Sweet and rich

ABOVE **'Spirit of Freedom'**

Description of foliage: Mid-green, crimson when young; semi-glossy
Height and spread: 8 x 6ft (2.5 x 2m)
This is a climbing rose in the style of a bourbon rose. It is thornless, and the blooms are bright cherry-pink, not especially shapely, but extremely freely borne. The scent is delicious and powerful. It is one of the first, and last roses to flower in the growing year. Unfortunately it is prone to blackspot, rust and mildew.

CLIMBING ROSES THAT PRODUCE HIPS

Most do produce the autumn fruits, but some are more attractive than others. Here are five of the best:
Rosa filipes 'Kiftsgate' Bright red autumn hips (see main entry).
Rosa helenae Large clusters of pure white flowers are followed in autumn by small orange, oval hips in their masses.
Rosa longicuspis A less hardy climber needing a sheltered wall; white flowers are followed by small orange-red hips.
'Mme Grégoire Staechelin' AGM Large orange hips (see main entry).
Rosa mulliganii A wild rambling-like rose with small white flowers and glossy red hips.

ABOVE **Rosa helenae**

Glossary

Balled A flower that does not open properly, and rots when still in bud.

Bare-root Plants sold with their roots bare of soil (i.e. not in a pot or container).

Boss Cluster of stamens at the centre of the rose flower.

Budding A form of grafting, where a bud is stripped off one plant (the scion) and grafted on to the rootstock of another.

Cultivar A cultivated plant that is clearly distinguished by one or more characteristics which it retains when propagated; a contraction of 'cultivated variety', and frequently abbreviated to 'cv.' in plant naming.

Deadheading The removal of spent flowers or flower heads.

Dieback Death of shoots, starting from the tips, and as a result of damage or disease.

Dog rose The common wild rose, *Rosa canina*, found in hedgerows throughout Europe, Asia and North America and Australia.

Double Referred to in flower terms as a bloom with several layers of petals; usually there would be a minimum of 20 petals. 'Very double' flowers have more than 40 petals.

Floribunda Bush rose producing rose flowers in clusters, or heads. These are generally hybrids between hybrid tea and polyantha roses.

Flush The period during which the rose bears its normal complement of blooms. There may be more than one flush per year.

Genus (plural genera) A category in plant naming, comprising a group of related species.

Graft Method of propagation by which an artificial union is made between a shoot or bud of one rose and the rootstock of another, so that they eventually function as one plant.

Graft union (or Union) The point on a plant stem at which the scion and rootstock are joined.

Ground cover Usually low-growing plants that grow over the soil, so suppressing weed growth.

Hardwood cutting Method of propagation by which a cutting is taken from mature wood at the end of the growing season.

Heeling in Laying plants in the soil, with the roots covered, as a temporary measure until full planting can take place.

Hip (sometimes 'Hep') The fruit of a rose; in some varieties these are large and decorative.

Hybrid The offspring of genetically different parents, usually produced in cultivation, but sometimes arising in the wild.

Hybrid tea Bush rose producing large flowers, usually single or in very small clusters.

Quartered A characteristic of some roses, particularly the older cultivars, where the flowers are roughly divided into quarters when they open out.

Rambler A trailing climbing rose, but usually with many more, smaller flowers.

Recurrent-flowering (see 'Repeat flowering')

Remontant A plant that flowers more than once during the growing season.

Repeat-flowering The production of two or more flushes during the growing season.

Reverse The side of the petal that faces away from the centre of the rose.

Root-ball The roots and surrounding soil or compost visible when a plant is removed from a pot.

Rootstock A plant used to provide the root system for a grafted plant.

Rosa The genus name to which all roses belong.

Rosette Flower shape characterized by radiating circles of petals.

Scion A shoot or bud cut from one plant to graft onto the rootstock of another.

Seedling A young plant that has developed, accidentally or intentionally, from a seed.

Semi-double Referred to in flower terms as a bloom with more than a single layer of petals; usually there are 10–20 petals.

Side shoot A stem that arises from the side of a main shoot or stem.

Single In flower terms, a single layer of petals opening out into a fairly flat shape, comprising no more than five petals.

Species A category in plant naming, the rank below genus, containing related, individual plants.

Sport A mutation, caused by a genetic change (accidental or intentional) which may produce shoots which have different characteristics, such as flowers of another colour.

Stamen(s) The male flower organ, which carries an anther (or anthers) that produce(s) pollen.

Standard Rose with a head of flowers on top of a single, tall stem, formed by grafting a desirable cultivar onto a stemmed rootstock. A rambler rose forms the 'head' of a weeping standard rose.

Sucker Generally a shoot that arises from below ground, emanating from a plant's roots, but it also refers to any shoot on a grafted plant that originates from below the graft union.

Truss A compact cluster of blooms, or fruits; often large and decorative.

Variety Botanically, this is a naturally occurring variant of a wild species; usually shorted to 'var.' in plant naming.

Underplanting Low-growing or ground-hugging plants which are planted beneath larger plants.

Wind-rock Destabilizing of a plant's roots by the wind.

About the author

Graham Clarke was born in a rose garden – literally. His father was in charge of the world-famous Queen Mary Rose Garden in London's Regent's Park, and at the time of his birth the family lived in a lodge within the garden. During his formative years he was surrounded by some 30,000 roses in dozens of large beds, which burst into life and colour every summer. This annual transformation was the cause not just of his life-long interest in roses, but also his entire love of gardens and gardening.

When he left school, Graham went to study with the Royal Horticultural Society at Wisley, in Southern England. He spent three months working in the rose garden there, and this gave him an even greater understanding and knowledge of the subject. After Wisley he worked as a gardener at Buckingham Palace in London – and again specialized in the rose garden, which contains more than 2,000 roses and some 60 different varieties. This very private rose garden is seen by Her Majesty the Queen on most of the days she is in residence.

For more than 20 years Graham has been a gardening writer and journalist. He has written seven books, and countless articles for most of the major UK gardening magazines. At various times he was editor of *Amateur Gardening* (the UK's leading weekly magazine for amateurs) and *Horticulture Week* (the UK's leading weekly magazine for professionals), and is now a freelance garden writer and consultant. He lives in Dorset, on England's south coast, with his wife, two daughters and numerous rose bushes.

Index

Pages highlighted in **bold** indicate photographs of plants.

GMC Publications Ltd, 166 High Street, Lewes, East Sussex BN7 1XU, United Kingdom
Tel: 01273 488005 Fax: 01273 402866
www.gmcbooks.com

Contact us for a complete catalogue, or visit our website.